INTRODUCTORY PSYCHOLOGY

CLEP* Test Study Guide

© 2021 Breely Crush Publishing, LLC

*CLEP is a registered trademark of the College Entrance Examination Board which does not endorse this book.

971010221143

Published by Breely Crush Publishing, LLC
10808 River Front Parkway
South Jordan, UT 84095
www.breelycrushpublishing.com

ISBN-10: 1-61433-642-3
ISBN-13: 978-1-61433-642-6

Printed and bound in the United States of America.

*CLEP is a registered trademark of the College Entrance Examination Board which does not endorse this book.

Table of Contents

Introduction

Congratulations! You've bought and are reading the best resource to passing your Introduction to Psychology CLEP test. CLEP tests are a great way to save time and money. If you learn the contents of this study guide, you should be able to pass the test. Before you get started though, you should learn what CLEP tests your college accepts for credit.

History of Psychology

Wilhelm Wundt created the first scientific psychology laboratory. In the 16th Century, Francis Bacon introduced the scientific method.

Psychological Approaches

Biological: This theory is based on biology. People who follow this school of thought believe that behavior and personality are linked to their genetics.

Behavioral: To study and observe behavior. Behaviorists see the individual as a blank slate upon which the impressions of experiences negative and positive can be recorded.

Cognitive: Cognitive theorists examine how the mind is involved in knowing, learning, remembering and thinking. They study how the mind relates to behavior.

Humanistic: Humanists believe that all people are inherently good and are motivated to achieve their full potential.

Psychoanalytical: This theory revolves around the individual's unconscious motivation.

Structuralism: Created by Wilhelm Wundt. The name comes from his investigation of the elements or "structures" of the mind. He emphasized the importance of the classification of the mind's structures and focused on conscious thought.

Functionalism: William James created this theory. He was interested in the "how" part of behavior. He thought our minds are a continuous flow of information about our experiences. He thought that psychology's role is to study the mind and behavior in adapting to the environment.

Nature vs. Nurture. Nature means that a child will be born with whatever disposition, tastes, and personality they were "meant" to have. There are bad seeds. Nurture means that all children are good; it is the way they are brought up that effects their personality and later, their actions. This is an ongoing debate between psychologists.

🎓 Research

To study the way that people grow, learn, adapt and interact with others, psychologists use a standardized method so that other people in the scientific community can understand their findings and agree on research.

Scientists use a specific vocabulary to conduct their research. A **participant** is a person that a scientist studies in their experiment. They can also be referred to as a subject. When a scientist is performing an experiment on an animal, they are also referred to as a subject or a participant.

When scientists want to study an entire city, culture, or population, they will use a sample. A **sample** is a small collection of subjects. The number of people you need to participate to make the sample the most accurate is statistically generated based on the amount of the population.

Everything that a scientist measures and studies is called a **variable**. For example, if you were conducting research on insomnia, you would have variables which include the amount of time it takes a person to fall asleep, how much caffeine they ingest, how much alcohol or drugs they ingest, what distractions are in the room, etc.

Research must meet four main tests:

1. Research must be **replicable**. Another scientist, given the information regarding the experiment, should be able to reproduce the experiment with the same results. This is how the scientific community accepts or rejects new theories. If the experiment can be reproduced several times by different people in different organizations or locations, it lends to its credibility. This means that the theory must be quantitative, or measurable and not qualitative. Qualitative means that something is similar in structure or organization but it cannot be measured in numerical terms.

2. The research must be **falsifiable**. This means that a theory has to be stated in a way that can be rejected or accepted. Think of it as asking a yes or no question. Is smoking bad for you? The answer is yes or no, and can be proven. This could be stated as "smoking is bad for you because it contains carcinogens." This is

a falsifiable statement. It needs to be stated this way so that it can be proved or disproved. If a researcher does not consider all the evidence, but ignores the information that does not prove their theory and accepts the information that proves it, they are showing **confirmation bias**.

3. The research must be precisely stated and conducted. A theory needs to be stated precisely so it can be replicated. Scientists use operational definitions to state exactly how a variable will be measured. For example, a researcher studying birth order may notice that children who are the oldest of several siblings tend to be more responsible as adults and parents. The researcher may conclude that this is because they have experienced more time nurturing and caring for younger siblings. In our birth order study, the scientist needs to find a way to measure "responsible." He or she might decide that they will use the individual's credit reports as an operational variable to show responsibility.

4. Researchers must use the most logical, simplest explanation possible as an answer to their theory. This is also called the **principle of parsimony** or **Occam's razor**.

THE SCIENTIFIC METHOD

The Scientific Method is the accepted way to conduct research. It contains several steps. First, a researcher created a hypothesis. This is the testable idea. Second, information is gathered through an experiment or research. This information either proves or disproves the theory which leads to the third step, refining the theory. At this point, it may be necessary to start the experiment all over, having applied the new information learned in the experiment. The fourth and final stage is developing a theory. Again, at this point, it is necessary to test the theory through the scientific method. Once a theory has been proved successfully by reputable researchers, the more times it is reproduced, the more credibility it has.

RESEARCH METHODS

Information for a theory or experiment can be gathered several ways.

Case Study

In a case study, a single individual (subject) is intensely studied. The researcher gets data through personal interview with the subject, its employees, neighbors, contacts, etc., and by reviewing documentation or records (i.e., medical history, family life, etc.). Other sources for information are testing and direct observation of the subject.

Survey

A survey is a great way to get information about a specific type of information. For example, a survey would work well to measure performance in an office environment.

These can be aggregated and used to improve employee performance. Usually with a survey, questionnaires are given out to participants who are then asked to answer questions to the best of their ability. When a participant fills out a survey themselves *about* themselves, it is called self-report data. This information can possibly not be as reliable as other research methods because subjects may be dishonest with their answers. For example, the question "Are you ever late to work?" may have respondents answering "no" when in fact, they are late but either do not remember that or are dishonest to avoid punishment or negative information about themselves. Many answer with the answers they feel that researchers (or themselves) want to hear instead of the truth.

Naturalistic Observation

Jean Piaget extensively used natural observation to study children. Naturalistic observation is when a researcher observes and studies subjects without interacting or interfering with them. Piaget observed the behavior of children playing in the schoolyard to access developmental stages. Another example well known to television viewers of the series "Star Trek" involves "The Prime Directive." This is the most perfect version demonstrated (in fiction) of naturalistic observation. In the show, the researchers had the ability to view and study human cultures without being known to the subjects because of their advancements in technology. In the series, it was a great violation to interact with and impact the development of these cultures and societies.

Laboratory Observation

Laboratory observation is conducted in a laboratory environment. This method is selected to monitor specific biological changes in individuals. In a lab setting, expensive and sophisticated machinery can be used to study the participants. Sometimes one-way mirrors are used to observe the participants.

Psychological Tests

Psychological tests give information about participants. Some of the more common include standardized tests such as the Minnesota Multiphasic Personality Inventory also known as the MMPI (a personality test), aptitudes, interests, etc. A participant's score is then compared to the norms for that test. A test is valid if it measures what it is supposed to. For example, a test on depression will be able to measure a person's depression. If it cannot, then the test is not valid. Content validity is applied when a test measures something with more that one facet. For example, a test for overall cooking skills would not be valid if it only tested baking cakes and not other skills such as grilling meat or making soup.

Cross Sectional Studies

When people of different ages are studied at one particular time it is called a cross sectional study, because you have a cross section of the population or demographic that you want to study.

Longitudinal Studies

Longitudinal studies are when people are followed and studied over a long period of time and check up on at certain points. These are best used to study the development of certain traits and track health issues. An example of a longitudinal study would be: 600 infants that were put up for adoption were tracked for several years. Some infants were adopted, some returned to the birth mothers and some were put into foster care. Which group adjusted the best and why?

Correlation Research

Correlation research is used to show links between events, people, actions, behaviors, etc. Correlation research does not determine the causes of behavior but is linked to statistics. Causation is the cause of something. Correlation is not causation. This is an example of FAULTY, incorrect causation: a child eats an ice cream three times a week. This child scores well on school aptitude tests. It is determined that eating ice cream will make you smarter and do better on tests. There are additional factors or many others including socioeconomic status resulting from educated parents who genetically pass on their aptitude for school as well as their influence on the importance of school. In this situation, it is most likely the parents who contribute to the child's aptitude scores.

When conducting a survey and you have completed compiling the data, you will be able to measure the correlation between certain traits and variables tested. A correlation coefficient measures the strength between the two variables. A correlation coefficient is a number between -1 and +1.

A positive correlation means that when one variable increases, the other variable increases as well. For example, the more a couple fights, the more likely they are to get a divorce.

When one variable increases and the other variable decreases it is called a negative correlation. An example of this would be babies that are held by their caregivers tend to cry less. When the amount of time they are held goes up, the time they cry goes down.

The higher the number of the correlation coefficient, the stronger the correlation. A +0.9 or -0.9 shows a very strong correlation because the number is closest to a whole positive number 1 or a whole negative number 1. A weak correlation is a +0.1 or a -0.1. A correlation of zero shows that there is no relationship between variables.

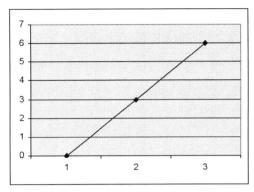

Positive correlation

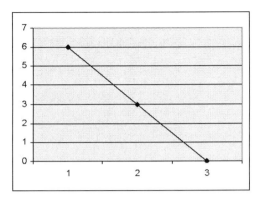

Negative correlation

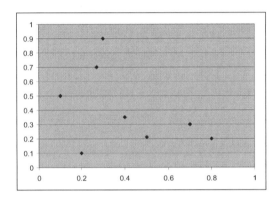

No correlation (above)

Census

A census is a collection of data from all cases or people in the chosen set. Usually, the most common form of a census would take place within an entire school of state. This means that every person of that school or state must be included. Censuses are usually not performed because they are so expensive. A census is valuable because it gives an accurate representation. To save time and money, survey companies will ask 1000 people or so (remember, the number changes based on the amount of people to be surveyed. A good rule of thumb is 10%). This is called sampling. For example, a recent census shows that the single person is the fastest-growing household type. So basically, a sample is a set of cases of people randomly chosen from a large group. The sample is to represent the group. The larger the sample, the more accurate the results.

READING CHARTS AND GRAPHS

Charts and graphs are easy ways to display information and make it easily readable.

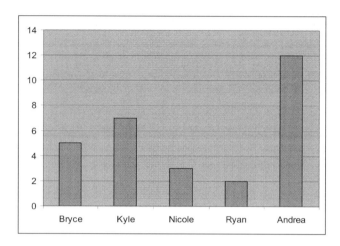

EXPERIMENTS

In experiments, a researcher manipulates variables to test theories and conclusions. Each experiment has independent and dependent variables. This is how researchers test cause and effect links and relationships.

The independent variable is the variable that researchers have direct control over. Dependent variable is then observed by the researcher.

In experiments, there are usually two groups of participants. One group is the experimental group and one group is the control group. The most common example is in medical trials. Let's say there is a trial run of a new diet drug. The researcher will split the group randomly in two. Group 1 will receive the diet pill that is being tested. Group 2 will receive a placebo pill. The placebo pill is simply a sugar pill. Group 2 will not know that they are not receiving the real drug. This allows the researchers to study the true effectiveness and side-effects of the pill. When the people are assigned to a group randomly, it is called **random assignment**. This particular experiment was a single-blind experiment. A **double-blind** experiment is when none of the doctors, researches and participants know who is getting the real drug. It is assigned by computer or an independent individual where it is kept confidential until the conclusion of the study.

When a participant starts to feel the effects of the drug but is *actually* taking a sugar pill or placebo it is called the **placebo effect**.

It is very important to avoid bias in research. Bias is the distortion of the results. Common types of bias include the sampling bias, subject bias and researcher bias. The placebo effect is an example of subject bias. Experimenter or researcher bias is avoided by conducting a double-blind experiment.

There are some disadvantages to experiments. They cannot be used to study everything. There are officially defined rules how humans and animals must be treated with the experiment. In an infamous experiment by psychologist Stanley Milgram, subjects were told that they were giving painful electric shocks to other people when in reality they were not. Some people consider this experiment unethical because it caused the participants emotional discomfort.

Researchers must get consent from their participants before conducting experiment. Informed consent means that the participants must know the content of the experiment and be warned of any risk or harm.

ANIMAL RESEARCH

Animal research has historically been a very important aspect of psychological studies. Basic principles of behavior and medical responses can both be tested effectively on animals to increase understanding and prepare them for human use. In the interest of protecting animals from abusive experiments, official guidelines have been developed by the American Psychological Association (APA).

These guidelines include aspects relating to obtaining, care, living conditions, and treatment of the animals. Animals used in psychological testing cannot be bred in laboratories, and must be obtained legally and humanely. It is also expected that experimentation will be as noninvasive and humane as possible. Experiments should be designed to allow for the least amount of suffering possible. Housing spaces for experimental animals are inspected twice a year, and are expected to meet or exceed regulatory standards. Euthanasia is allowed only if it is the most humane option.

INTERPRETING DATA

The "Mean" is also referred to as the "Arithmetic Mean".

The Arithmetic Mean is calculated by finding the **sum** of all "N" values and dividing by n N. This is the general formula to calculate the arithmetic mean: $\dfrac{\sum_{i=1}^{n} X_i}{N}$

Example of Arithmetic Mean:

What is the arithmetic mean of the numbers 10, 8, 6, 12, and 9?

X = (10 + 8 + 6 + 12 + 9) = 45 and N = 5 because there 5 numbers in the list.

Therefore, $\dfrac{X}{N} = \dfrac{76}{8} = \mathbf{9}$

What is the "Mode"? The Mode is the number that appears the most number of times in the sample data.

For example, the Mode for the following set of data {10, 12, 14, 10, 8, 10, 7} is **10** because 10 appears the most number of times in the data set.

What is the "Median"? The Median is the middle value or the arithmetic mean of the middle values. The following example will demonstrate how to find the Median.

Sample Data = {3, 3, 5, 6, 7, 9, 10, 12, 14}

The Median = 7 because it has four numbers to the left of it and four numbers to the right of it in the sample data.

> NOTE: The data MUST be in numerical order to find the Median. For example, if you are given a sample data set of {5, 6, 12, 3, 3, 10, 7, 14, 9} you must first put it in numerical order: {3, 3, 5, 6, 7, 9, 10, 12, 14} to find the correct Median of 7.

Find the Median for the following set of numbers: {2, 3, 4, 5, 6, 7}

Since there is an even number of numbers in the data set you will need to find the arithmetic mean of the two middle numbers 4 & 5. (4+5)/2 = 4.5. Therefore, the Median is 4.5.

What is the "Range"? The Range is simply the difference between the largest data value and the smallest data value. For example, the Range in the set of {2, 4, 7, 8, 10, 12, 24} is 24-2 = **22.**

What is "Standard Deviation"? Standard Deviation relates data points to the Mean of the sample data set.

Standard Deviation (s) is calculated using: $s = \sqrt{\dfrac{\sum\limits_{i=1}^{n}(X_i - \bar{X})^2}{N}}$

Where $\bar{X}$ = the Arithmetic Mean of the data set

X_i = the value of each number in the data set

N = Number of values in the data set

Example of Standard Deviation: Find the Standard Deviation of the following set of numbers: {12, 6, 7, 3, 15, 10, 18, 5}.

$$\bar{X} = \frac{12+6+7+3+15+10+18+5}{8} = \frac{76}{8} = 9.5$$

$$s = \sqrt{\frac{(12-9.5)^2 + (6-9.5)^2 + (7-9.5)^2 + (3-9.5)^2 + (15-9.5)^2 + (10-9.5)^2 + (18-9.5)^2 + (5-9.5)^2}{8}}$$

Therefore, $\sqrt{23.75} = 4.87$

Clinical Research: This is research done with a control group and a treatment group. A good example of this is a diet pill. A clinical research trial will have two groups of people who all think they are taking this drug to help them lose weight. They are all monitored and report their progress and symptoms to researchers. One group, the control group, is not given the drug. Those persons thinking they are on the drug may still lose weight because of their positive thinking or other thoughts or outside influences. Sometimes a study is called a blind or double blind study. In a blind trial, the patients do not know they are taking the placebo. In a double blind study, neither the patient nor the doctor knows who is taking the real medicine and who is taking the placebo. This helps maintain the highest accuracy.

Correlational Research: Correlational research is used to find the amount that one variable changes in relation to another. For example, is there a correlation between IQ results and grades? Correlation can be positive or negative in results.

Clinical Psychologist: Usually has a doctoral degree in psychology plus an internship. They cannot prescribe medicine.

Psychiatrist: A medical doctor with a degree who specializes in psychotherapy. Psychiatrists can prescribe drugs.

Ethics: Principals and standards of behavior, including morals. Determining what is right or wrong and having one's actions correlate with one's beliefs.

Endocrine System

The endocrine system is made up of the **hypothalamus** and other endocrine glands. Endocrine glands create and release chemicals into the bloodstream. The **pituitary gland** releases hormones that regulate the hormone secretions of other glands. The pituitary gland is located at the base of the skull and is about the size of a pea. Adrenal glands affect our moods, energy level and stress. Adrenal glands also secrete epinephrine (adrenaline) and norepinephrine.

The nervous system has an area called the **Autonomic Nervous System (ANS).** ANS works as an involuntary system; usually, we don't know it is there. Other involuntary systems include respiratory and cardiac functions. Here's the test: if you have to think about doing it, it's not involuntary. ANS is most important in the "fight or flight" response. When we experience large amounts of stress such as in an emergency, our body gives us extra energy (adrenaline) to fight, perhaps against an attacker, or to take flight, to run from the attacker. In non-stress times, this system allows us to rest and digest. This system is broken up into three different areas. These are:

- **sympathetic nervous system**
- arousing part of the system **parasympathetic nervous system**
- calming part of the system

Limbic System: Structures in the cerebral cortex related to memory and emotion.

Hippocampus: Located in the limbic system. Its primary function is to store memories.

Cerebral cortex: The most developed part of the brain. Largest part of the brain (80%). Underneath the cerebral cortex are four lobes of the brain. These are:

- Occipital lobe: related to vision
- Temporal lobe: hearing
- Frontal lobe: voluntary muscles and intelligence
- Parietal lobe: body sensations

Brain

The brain is a part of the central nervous system. It controls all necessary functions of the body. All emotions originate in the brain as well as memory and thought processes.

It interprets signals from other parts of the body and turns those signals into rational thought such as, "My leg hurts from running too much." This developed brain is what makes us human by controlling our emotions, thoughts and consciousness.

The brain is located in the skull. The skull protects this organ. There are also other things that protect the brain. There are three membranes that shield it. The outer layer, the dura mater, is the strongest and thickest. Beneath that layer is another membrane, called the arachnoid layer. Beneath that is the final layer, the pia mater, which is mostly blood vessels. A clear fluid called cerebrospinal fluid covers the entire brain and is used to transport chemicals through the brain and to regulate pressure.

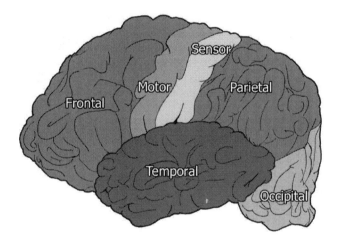

The brain and the spinal cord make up the central nervous system. The **Cerebrum** is the two large halves of the brain that you can see on the left. The deep "crack" in the middle is called the longitudinal fissure. The two halves of the brain communicate via bundles of axons called commissures. The largest commissure is called the corpus callosum.

Cerebrum: Houses memories and controls our responses to different sensory signals.

Cerebellum: Coordinates all movements and muscles.

Pons: Control breathing and heart rate.

Brain Stem: Sends commands to all other parts of the body.

Thalamus: Main relay station for incoming sensory signals to cerebral cortex and outgoing motor signals from it. All the senses but **smell** report to the thalamus.

Hypothalamus: Regulates internal temperature, eating, sleeping, drinking, emotions, and sexual activity.

Questions on the functions of the brain make up an extremely large amount of the material on the test. Make certain you understand all the workings of it.

Right Brain/Left Brain

Many people think that if you are "left brained" then you have a higher aptitude in math and science, as thinking is supposedly more analytical in that area. The "right" half of the brain is supposedly where creativity and art come from. This is a myth. Something important you need to know is the left half of the brain controls the right hand, right eye, and speech. The right half of the brain controls the left hand, left eye and simple comprehension.

Genetics

Gregor Mendel was the father of genetics and inheritance. He was a priest in charge of a garden who got interested in some of the plants. Pea pods are self-fertilizing. Three of four seeds were purple; one seed out of four was white. Each plant contained two genetic codes. The purple was dominant over white because it showed up more often. Look at the chart below to determine the chances of getting each kind of plant:

PP=Purple (Upper case means dominant, lower case means recessive)
pp=White

	Purple	White
Purple	PP	P*p*
White	*p*P	*pp*

The inheritance of sex is determined by the x and the y chromosome. All chromosomes come in pairs. For use in the chart, females are XX and males are XY.

	X	X
X	XX	XX
Y	YX	YX

To get the values (YX), all you do is add the intersection of each row and column on the table. According to the table above (and biology) the chances of having either a boy or girl are 50%.

Chromosomes in DNA carry genes.

Somatic Cell is a full set of chromosomes (there is a total of 46 chromosomes, thus 46 genes). **Cloning** is done by creating reproduction using only the somatic cell.
Gametes are the reproductive cells (eggs and sperm). Each has exactly one-half a set of normal chromosomes; this is why you need one of each to conceive. Gametes fuse together to make a zygote. A **zygote** is the first part of a human. Only a few genes are on the "y" chromosome. All genes on the "y" are passed on to boys *every time*, but never to girls.

Sexuality

The following terminology will be helpful for you to know for the test.

Sexual Identity: recognition of ourselves as sexual beings; a mix of gender identity, gender roles and orientation.

Gonads: the reproductive organs in a male (testes) or females (ovaries)

Puberty: the period of sexual maturation

Pituitary gland: the gland that controls the release of hormones from the gonads
Gender: your sense of being a man or a woman as defined by your society **Gender roles:** expression of your male or femaleness on daily basis

Gender-role stereotypes: generalizations about each gender. For example, men are aggressive and more logical. Women are more nurturing and emotional.

Socialization: process by which a society identifies its expectations

Sexual Orientation: a person's attraction to other people

STDs: Sexually Transmitted Diseases which include AIDS and Herpes.

Heterosexual: attraction to the opposite sex

Homosexual: attraction to the same sex

Bisexual: attraction to both sexes

Homophobia: irrational hatred and or fear of homosexuals **Celibacy:** not being involved in a sexual relationship **Autoerotic behavior:** sexual self-stimulation, masturbation

Erogenous zones: areas of the body which, when touched, lead to sexual arousal.

Four stages of the sexual response:

1. Excitement phase
2. Plateau phase
3. Orgasm phase
4. Resolution phase

Human papilloma virus or HPV is considered to be the most common sexually transmitted infections worldwide. This virus is believed to cause most cases of cervical cancer, the second most common cancer for women. Gardasil is an FDA approved vaccine for HPV in women. It is only effective before contracting the virus, and hasn't yet been approved as a vaccine for men.

Vasocongestion is when there is increased blood flow to an area of the body causing an increase in blood pressure and swelling of tissue. Vasocongestion is essential to human sexuality because it is what causes the penis to become erect. However, it also has other applications. For example, blushing is one type of vasocongestion.

Memory & Attention

Memory is made up of three parts: encoding the information; representation of the information; and retrieving of what was previously stored in memory. **Selective attention** is focusing attention on a small amount of information. Attention can be selective just like hearing. Sometimes it is hard to hear or pay attention to ideas or thoughts that don't resonate with our goals or actions.

 *Sight*

The vestibular sense is the sense that gives information about balance and body movement. It tells you if your body is moving, tilting, shaking, etc. **Absolute threshold:** How much sensation do you have to experience to feel a feather brush your skin? Each person has an absolute threshold that is the minimum amount of something we can detect or sense.

Sclera: White part of the eye that protects and manages the shape of the eye.

Iris: Ring of muscles that make up the colored part of the eye.

Pupil: The part of the eye that looks black is the opening of the iris. It opens and closes to let the correct amount of light enter the eye.

Cornea: A clear membrane in front of the eye that protects it.

Lens: It is transparent and is located in the front of the eye.

The cornea and the lens are responsible for bending the light falling on the eye and focusing it in the back of the eye. To help the eye focus, the lens changes its curves. This process is called **accommodation.** The **retina** is in the back of the eye and is light sensitive. It includes receptors called cones and rods and other neurons. Receptors are important for the ability to see. Rods (each is a receptor) are very sensitive to light but do not help with color vision. Cones are what we use to view colors. There are three types of cones used to determine colors by comparing the results between the three cones. There is only one type of rod so it is not helpful in determining color, as it has nothing to compare to.

Eyes are necessary to enables us to have depth perception. Depth perception allows to us judge the amount of distance between ourselves and an object. The brain processes certain facts in order to calculate the distance. Some of these cues only require the use of one eye, and are referred to as monocular (mono for one) cues.

Size: If two objects are the same relative size, the one that is slightly larger will be perceived as being closer.

Texture: The farther away an object goes into the distance, the less distinct the texture.

Motion parallax: When moving, objects closer to you seem to move faster than objects far away.

Aerial perspective: Objects that are farther away seem to be less distinct and more blurred.

Linear perspective: Parallel lines seem to meet in the distance.

Overlap: When one object covers another, the one in front seems to be closest, the one behind, farther away.

Binocular vision is the ability to use both eyes to see and overlap their vision paths, without having double vision.

Hearing

The Auditory System is another term for hearing. Sound is another way that we get information about our environment. Sounds or sound waves are vibrations in the air that we receive through the ear and are processed by our hearing system.

Noise: Irrelevant stimuli that compete for our attention (traffic, for example).

Frequency: The number of full wavelengths that pass through a point in a given amount of time.

Pitch: The ear's interpretation of a sound's frequency (e.g., notes in a musical song).

Amplitude: Amplitude is the amount of pressure produced by a sound wave and is measured in dB or decibels.

Loudness: A sound wave's amplitude.

Timbre: The tone color or perceptual quality of a sound.

Outer ear: Includes the pinna and the external auditory canal.

Middle ear: Area of the ear with three main parts: eardrum, anvil and stirrup.

Inner ear: Oval window, cochlea, organ of Corti.

Cochlea: A fluid-filled structure in the inner ear that looks like a snail.

Organ of Corti: A part of the ear inside the cochlea. Contains sensors that change energy into impulses that are decoded by the brain.

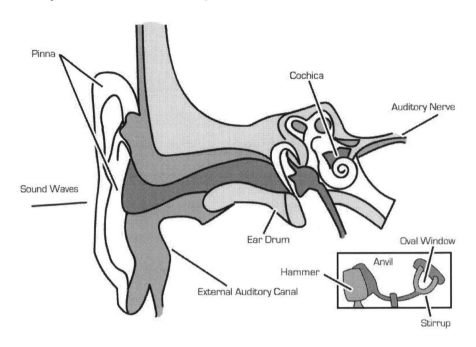

Taste and Smell

Taste is an important sense. On top of the tongue are papillae that are bumps that contain the taste buds. The taste buds recognize taste in four areas that are sweet, bitter, salty, and sour.

Smell is also an important sense. Smell can trigger emotion and memories. The scientific name for the sense of smell is the olfactory sense. A person can smell something, like food, when airborne molecules of an odor reach tiny receptor cells in the nasal cavity. The olfactory epithelium, located at the top of the nasal cavity, is where the receptor cells are located for smell. These receptor cells have hair-like antennae that make contact with the air, which help us smell.

The partial or complete loss of smell is known as anosmia. Although anosmia isn't generally a sign of bigger or more dangerous problems, it is inconvenient because of the importance of smell. Smell is necessary for an individual to properly taste food and to be aware of potential dangers such as gas leaks. Partial loss of smell is a common side effect of colds and sinus infections. When this is the case it typically goes away with time. However, anosmia can also be permanent. More permanent causes of anosmia include chemical exposure, old age, Alzheimer's, brain damage, or physical defects such as bones or tumors blocking the nasal passage.

🎓 Touch

Galvanic skin response, or GSR, is a measure of the electrical impulses in the skin. These impulses have a measurable change based on the intensity and type of emotions that a person is experiencing. GSR is used most commonly in polygraph (lie detector) tests. The tests work because when a person becomes anxious, angry or aroused the autonomic nervous system automatically responds with changes in blood pressure or temperature. These changes affect the conductivity or resistance of the skin. By measuring the GSR in a polygraph test these changes can become powerful signs that a person is lying.

🎓 Perception

Perception is the way that the brain organizes and gives meaning to the information provided by the senses. Perception processes have four characteristics that are:

- Automatic: you do not have to think about it. It happens automatically.

- Selective: you may be more interested in a cute boy rather than what he is saying.

- Contextual: perception is contextual. If you have heard a movie is scary, you may be more inclined to get scared.

- Creative: perception fills in areas that we do not have complete information about. For example, when a friend's face is partially blocked by their hair, your mind fills in the blanks about how their face looks underneath the hair.

Gestalt psychology is an approach that assumes that people organize their perceptions by patterns. They believe in the principle of closure. When someone sees an incomplete form, they fill in the pieces. See below:

Your eyes and mind interpret this to be a triangle, when in fact, it is just a line. This is an example of the "principle of closure".

Depth perception is what makes a person able to see objects as they are, in three dimensions. It is what causes some items to look farther away or close up. We see depth by using two kinds of cues. These cues are called binocular cues and monocular cues. Binocular cues are cues made with both eyes. Monocular cues are made by each eye working alone.

 The **Visual Cliff** shows that infants have depth perception. This is a study that was done by having infants placed on a solid, opaque surface. The infant's mothers were placed at the end of the table, where the opaque surface disappeared and glass began. The infants did not want to cross the glass because they could see the distance between where they were and the floor.

Consciousness

Consciousness is an awareness. This includes an awareness of external events, which are things that happen outside of your body. Internal events are things that happen inside your body such as internal thoughts about your emotions and body functions. William James thought of the mind as a stream of consciousness, a flow of emotions, sensations and thoughts. Contrastingly, Freud believed the unconscious motivates our actions (through the id, ego and superego).

Sometimes we have daydreams. Daydreaming is another form of consciousness that involves very little effort. It is like dreaming while we are awake. Letting your mind wander is a form of daydreaming.

When people take drugs, their mind is in an altered state of consciousness. Other states of consciousness include meditation, trauma, hypnosis, fatigue, etc.

 Sleep

We all need sleep in order to function properly. But the real question in why? Scientists have several theories on why this is necessary. Sleep helps the body conserve energy. Sleep also repairs and restores body tissues that are depleted throughout the day, especially lean muscle tissue.

Sleep has four stages.

STAGE 1

Stage one begins when you just barely have fallen asleep. This stage only lasts a few minutes. The brain shows alpha and theta waves. Your muscles and pulse relax while your body temperature drops slightly.

STAGE 2

Stage two lasts around 20 minutes while the brain produces short bursts of brain waves.

STAGE 3 AND STAGE 4

Stage three and four are only about 30 minutes combined. In stages three and four, subjects are difficult to wake.

In a given night, a person experiences four complete sleep cycles. The order of the sleep cycles is as follows 1 2 3 4 3 2 REM. The body progresses through the cycles 1-4 then backwards until it reaches REM which replaces stage 1.

Once your body has reached stage four it enters REM or Rapid Eye Movement sleep. REM is the deep sleep which is also known as paradoxical sleep. It typically takes about 90 minutes to reach REM sleep. Dreams during REM sleep are the most vivid and the genital regions can show signs of sexual arousal.

During the end of Stage 4 sleep bed-wetting and sleep walking are most common.

Although every person needs a different amount of sleep per night, the range is usually between 6 and 9 hours per night. Studies have been performed on subjects who have not received enough REM sleep. These subjects are wakened when they have reached REM throughout the night. Their bodies later in the following days of the week will increase their REM cycle to make up for lost time, known as the REM rebound effect.

Sleep is affected by changes in the body. There are three types of biological rhythms that exist in everyone:

- Circadian rhythms: a cycle that completes in 24 hours.
- Infradian rhythms: any biological cycle that takes longer than 24 hours such as a women's menstrual cycle which occurs every 28 days.
- Ultradian rhythms: cycles that occur more than once per day.

Sleeping patterns also fluctuate with age. Babies spend most of their first months in sleep while the older a person gets, the less amount of sleep they require. However, sleeping too much can be a sign of depression.

Everyone occasionally has trouble sleeping. However, when you consistently cannot sleep at night or fall asleep but keep waking up, you could be suffering from insomnia. Insomnia disrupts the stages of the sleep cycle.

When a person experiences insomnia, he or she may enter a sleep clinic where they spend the night in a lab. The clinicians can use the following to measure the body's functions during sleep:

- EEGs (Electroencephalographs): brain waves

- EMGs (Electromyographs): muscle activity

- EOGs (Electrooculographs): eye movement

- EKGs (Electrocardiographs): heart activity

Another disorder affecting sleep is sleep apnea. Sleep apnea is when people stop breathing several times during the night and wake up gasping for air. Because they are being constantly roused from sleep, they may be unable to get all the REM sleep that they need to function properly.

Narcolepsy, another sleeping disorder, is when people fall asleep during the day. Narcolepsy can result in people falling asleep while driving, walking, etc. Sleep walking is when someone who is in fact asleep walks through their house, neighborhood, sits in their car, or talks to their companion. Because the person is actually asleep, they most likely will not remember anything when woken up.

Sleep apnea is a common disorder in which you have one or more pauses in breathing or shallow breaths while you sleep. Breathing pauses can last from a few seconds to a few minutes. They may occur as many as 30 times or more in an hour. Usually, normal breathing then starts again, sometimes with a loud snort or choking sound.

Sleep apnea usually is an ongoing condition that disrupts sleep. When breathing pauses or becomes shallow, you'll often move out of deep sleep and into light sleep. As a result, the quality of sleep is poor, which results in tiredness during the day. Sleep apnea is a leading cause of excessive daytime sleepiness.

 **Dreams**

Why do we dream? While no one knows for sure, there are several different ideas that people posses. For example, Freud believed that dreams express unconscious desires that society or individuals would find unacceptable in real life. Others believe that dreams are simply the by-product of the brain while it strengthens or weakens neurons. Another group believes that dreams are the brain's way of working out problems and scenarios while we sleep. For example, if you are giving a presentation at school, you may dream about different ways to present it or different ways it could go wrong.

During sleep, the brain's neurons activate and fire. The activation-synthesis theory explains that these random firings create dreams.

Hypnosis

Hypnosis is a more than just a trick to a stand up comedy show. During hypnosis, the mind becomes very open to the power of suggestion. Not everyone can become hypnotized either. Hypnosis can help the body to relax. It can be used successfully to help people lose weight, stop smoking, etc. It cannot force people to do things against their will, but will lower inhibitions so they may do things that they might not normally do. After a person has been hypnotized, it they are told to forget what has transpired, they will believe they have no memory of it. This is called posthypnotic amnesia.

Ernest Hilgard had the idea that hypnosis divides a person's consciousness into two parts. One half responds to the outside world while the other half may observe but it will not participate. However, many other researchers simply believe that a hypnotized person simply acts as they think a hypnotized person should.

The Big Five

The Big Five is the most widely used and accepted model of personality. It refers to five main personality types including agreeableness, conscientiousness, extroversion, neuroticism, and openness. The acronyms OCEAN and CANOE both represent the five personality traits. It is commonly used in the workplace and in creating effective teams. An employer can use the assessment to determine the traits that a potential employee has that are useful to them, that suit the needs of the job, and that work well with the other employees. Teams with similar personality profiles based on the big five tend to work well together.

The personality types are assessed by taking a test with questions that relate to one or more of the Big Five. The test for the personality types typically contains questions such as "I am easily distracted," "I am a private person" or "I enjoy meeting new people" which are answered on a scale ranging from "strongly agree" to "strongly disagree." A person can test high, mid-range, or low in each individual trait. A very high or very low score in a trait represents a strong personality indicator, and a mid-range score represents being neutral or average. For example, a high score in extroversion indicates an outgoing and energetic person, a mid-range score indicates average social inclination, and a low score indicates solitary and reserved person. Each trait similarly ranges from two opposite personality types. Descriptions of the Big Five traits are as follows:

Openness (inventive/curious vs. consistent/cautious)
Openness describes a person who is imaginative, insightful, curious, thinks out-of-the-box, and has a broad range of interests.

Conscientiousness (efficient/organized vs. easy-going/careless)
Conscientiousness describes a person who is thoughtful, goal-oriented, detail-oriented, organized, and self-disciplined.

Extraversion (outgoing/energetic vs. solitary/reserved)
Extraversion describes a person who is sociable, talkative, assertive, emotionally expressive, and energetic.

Agreeableness (friendly/compassionate vs. analytical/detached)
Agreeableness describes a person who is trusting, altruistic, kind, affectionate, compassionate, and cooperative.

Neuroticism (sensitive/nervous vs. secure/confident)
Neuroticism describes a person who is sensitive and easily expresses anxiety, anger, irritability, and sadness.

Pharmacology Principles

Each drug affects each person in a different way. Why? Here are the steps that are taken to product the desired result, for example, pain medication to a chronic arthritis sufferer.

1. A specific drug with a specific chemical structure is chosen to be used
2. The chosen drug is then measured to a certain quantity
3. Once measured, the drug is administered any number of ways (ex. orally, injection)
4. The drug is then absorbed into the blood stream and sent to the site of the action (in this case, the joints)

How effective the drug is depends on characteristics of the person and how that person reacts with the drugs. Some factors which can contribute to the effectiveness of the drug are:

- Race
- Age
- Weight
- Gender
- Drug tolerance
- Metabolism

The effect of the drug depends on how much is taken. A drug's dose is calculated based on a person's body weight. To administer the correct amount, first you must determine what the dose is equivalent to in milligrams per kilogram of body weight. Next, you need the weight of the patient in kilograms. For example, if the weight of the patient is 90kg and the dose is .10mg per kg, you would multiply the dose amount by the weight – .10kg X 90 = 9 mg of the drug.

What are the ways to administer drugs?

- Oral
- Subcutaneous (beneath the skin)
- Intramuscular (in muscle)
- Intravenous (directly into veins)
- Mucous membranes (inhalation, under the tongue, snorting or sniffing through nose)

The Dose-Response Curve

The Dose-Response Curve is a tool or chart that shows the effect of different doses resulting in different effects. Shown here is a typical dose-response curve. Basically, the higher the dose, the larger the effect.

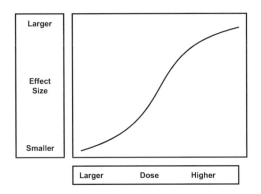

Biphasic drug effects look like the following. The dose response curve depends on the effect of a drug being measured. Each graph can measure a different effect. Maximal effect is the peak, or the point where the drug has the absolute most effect. Drug potency is the dose of a drug that yields the maximum effect. Metabolism is the way the body breaks down matter into simpler compounds, separating what the body needs from waste. A person's metabolism can affect the effectiveness of drugs, if the body metabolizes the drug too quickly or not quickly enough, it can effect the way the drug works.

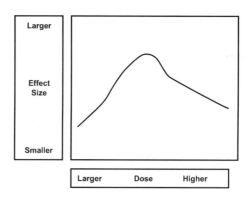

If a person regularly takes a drug, they can develop a tolerance to the drug. Tolerance means that as time goes on the drug will not be as effective to the person because their body has adapted to it. Therefore, to get the same effect, they will need more of the drug. Tolerance can be developed with illicit drugs, over the counter drugs like headache or cold medicine as well as with drugs such as coffee and caffeine.

A person may experience withdrawal when they are accustomed to using a particular drug for a period of time and then stop. Withdrawal symptoms differ with the type of drug.

If a person is dependent on a drug, they can experience two types of dependence; physical dependence and psychological dependence. With physical dependence, the withdrawal symptoms are real and the drug must be taken to avoid them. With psychological dependence, a person simply takes the drug to stop cravings or temptations. Drugs can be both psychologically and physically addictive.

Depressants

Historically, people of almost every culture have used chemical agents to induce sleep, relieve stress, and allay anxiety. While alcohol is one of the oldest and most universal agents used for these purposes, hundreds of substances have been developed that produce central nervous system depression. These drugs have been referred to as downers, sedatives, hypnotics, minor tranquilizers, anxiolytics, and anti-anxiety medications. Unlike most other classes of drugs of abuse, depressants are rarely produced in clandestine laboratories. Generally, legitimate pharmaceutical products are diverted to the illicit market. A notable exception to this is a relatively recent drug of abuse, gamma hydroxybutyric acid (GHB).

Choral hydrate and paraldehyde are two of the oldest pharmaceutical depressants still in use today. Other depressants, including gluthethimide, methaqualone, and meprobamate, have been important players in the milieu of depressant use and abuse. However, two major groups of depressants have dominated the licit and illicit market for nearly a century, first barbiturates and now benzodiazepines.

Barbiturates were very popular in the first half of the 20th century. In moderate amounts, these drugs produce a state of intoxication that is remarkably similar to alcohol intoxication. Symptoms include slurred speech, loss of motor coordination, and impaired judgment. Depending on the dose, frequency, and duration of use, one can rapidly develop tolerance, and physical and psychological dependence on barbiturates. With the development of tolerance, the margin of safety between the effective dose and the lethal dose becomes very narrow. That is, in order to obtain the same level of intoxication, the tolerant abuser may raise his or her dose to a level that may result in coma or death. Although many individuals have taken barbiturates therapeutically without harm, concern about the addiction potential of barbiturates and the ever-increasing number of fatalities associated with them led to the development of alternative medications. Today, less than 10 percent of all depressant prescriptions in the United States are for barbiturates.

Benzodiazepines were first marketed in the 1960s. Touted as much safer depressants with far less addiction potential than barbiturates, today these drugs account for about one out of every five prescriptions for controlled substances. Although benzodiazepines produce significantly less respiratory depression than barbiturates, it is now recognized that benzodiazepines share many of the undesirable side effects of the barbiturates. A number of toxic central nervous system effects are seen with chronic high-dose benzodiazepine therapy, including headaches, irritability, confusion, memory impairment, and depression. The risk of developing over-sedation, dizziness, and confusion increases substantially with higher doses of benzodiazepines. Prolonged use can lead to physical dependence even at doses recommended for medical treatment. Unlike barbiturates, large doses of benzodiazepines are rarely fatal unless combined with other drugs or alcohol. Although primary abuse of benzodiazepines is well documented, abuse of these drugs usually occurs as part of a pattern of multiple drug abuse. For example, heroin or cocaine abusers will use benzodiazepines and other depressants to augment their "high" or alter the side effects associated with over-stimulation or narcotic withdrawal.

There are marked similarities among the withdrawal symptoms seen with most drugs classified as depressants. In the mildest form, the withdrawal syndrome may produce insomnia and anxiety, usually the same symptoms that initiated the drug use. With a greater level of dependence, tremors and weakness are also present, and in its most severe form, the withdrawal syndrome can cause seizures and delirium. Unlike the withdrawal syndrome seen with most other drugs of abuse, withdrawal from depressants can be life threatening.

BARBITURATES

Barbiturates are classified as drugs which depress a person's system. They are grouped in three types, based on how fast acting they are. The first group, short acting, takes effect very quickly. Usually within around 20 minutes. They are generally used as types of anesthesia. The second group, intermediate acting, take longer to take effect, but last for a longer time. For example, an intermediate barbiturate may not take effect for 30 minutes, but will last for 6 hours. The third group is long acting. These drugs take hours or days to take effect, but are used long term, for example anxiety medication. Barbiturates have been replaced over time by benzodiazepines because of their addictive properties, and because they have more severe effects when overdose occurs.

Barbiturates were first introduced for medical use in the early 1900s. More than 2,500 barbiturates have been synthesized, and at the height of their popularity, about 50 were marketed for human use. Today, about a dozen are in medical use. Barbiturates produce a wide spectrum of central nervous system depression, from mild sedation to coma, and have been used as sedatives, hypnotics, anesthetics, and anticonvulsants. The primary differences among many of these products are how fast they produce an effect and how long those effects last. Barbiturates are classified as ultrashort, short, intermediate, and long-acting.

The ultrashort-acting barbiturates produce anesthesia within about one minute after intravenous administration. Those in current medical use are the Schedule IV drug methohexital (Brevital®), and the Schedule III drugs thiamyl (Surital®) and thiopental (Pentothal®). Barbiturate abusers prefer the Schedule II short-acting and intermediate-acting barbiturates that include amobarbital (Amytal®), pentobarbital (Nembutal®), secobarbital (Seconal®), and Tuinal (an amobarbital/secobarbital combination product). Other short and intermediate-acting barbiturates are in Schedule III and include butalbital (Fiorina®), butabarbital (Butisol®), talbutal (Lotusate®), and aprobarbital (Alurate®). After oral administration, the onset of action is from 15 to 40 minutes, and the effects last up to six hours. These drugs are primarily used for insomnia and preoperative sedation. Veterinarians use pentobarbital for anesthesia and euthanasia.

Long-acting barbiturates include phenobarbital (Luminal®) and mephobarbital (Mebaral®), both of which are in Schedule IV. Effects of these drugs are realized in about one hour and last for about 12 hours, and are used primarily for daytime sedation and the treatment of seizure disorders.

BENZODIAZEPINES

The benzodiazepine family of depressants is used therapeutically to produce sedation, induce sleep, relieve anxiety and muscle spasms, and to prevent seizures. In general, benzodiazepines act as hypnotics in high doses, anxiolytics in moderate doses, and sedatives in low doses. Of the drugs marketed in the United States that affect central nervous system function, benzodiazepines are among the most widely prescribed medications. Fifteen members of this group are presently marketed in the United States, and about 20 additional benzodiazepines are marketed in other countries. Benzodiazepines are controlled in Schedule IV of the CSA.

Short-acting benzodiazepines are generally used for patients with sleep-onset insomnia (difficulty falling asleep) without daytime anxiety. Shorter-acting benzodiazepines used to manage insomnia include estazolam (ProSom®), flurazepam (Dalmane®), temazepam (Restoril®), and triazolam (Halcion®). Midazolam (Versed®), a short-acting benzodiazepine, is utilized for sedation, or treating anxiety and amnesia in critical care settings and prior to anesthesia. It is available in the United States as an injectable preparation and as a syrup (primarily for pediatric patients).

Benzodiazepines with a longer duration of action are utilized to treat insomnia in patients with daytime anxiety. These benzodiazepines include alprazolam (Xanax®), chlordiazepoxide (Librium®), clorazepate (Tranxene®), diazepam (Valium®), halazepam (Paxipam®), lorzepam (Ativan®), oxazepam (Serax®), prazepam (Centrax®), and quazepam (Doral®). Clonazepam (Klonopin®), diazepam, and clorazepate are also used as anticonvulsants.

Benzodiazepines are classified in the CSA as depressants. Repeated use of large doses or, in some cases, daily use of therapeutic doses of benzodiazepines is associated with amnesia, hostility, irritability, and vivid or disturbing dreams, as well as tolerance and physical dependence. The withdrawal syndrome is similar to that of alcohol and may require hospitalization. Abrupt cessation of benzodiazepines is not recommended and tapering-down the dose eliminates many of the unpleasant symptoms of withdrawal.

Given the millions of prescriptions written for benzodiazepines, relatively few individuals increase their dose on their own initiative or engage in drug-seeking behavior. Those individuals who do abuse benzodiazepines often maintain their drug supply by getting prescriptions from several doctors, forging prescriptions, or buying diverted pharmaceutical products on the illicit market. Abuse is frequently associated with adolescents and young adults who take benzodiazepines to obtain a "high." This intoxicated state results in reduced inhibition and impaired judgment. Concurrent use of alcohol or other depressant with benzodiazepines can be life threatening. Abuse of benzodiazepines is particularly high among heroin and cocaine abusers. A large percentage of people entering treatment for narcotic or cocaine addiction also report abusing benzodiazepines. Alprazolam and diazepam are the two most frequently encountered benzodiazepines on the illicit market.

Benzodiazepines are any type of drug which is used to counter anxiety. Examples include Valium, Xanax, and Ativan. Benzodiazepines are considered to be the most abused pharmaceutical drug. Although benzodiazepines overdoses do not generally cause severe complications, it is unwise to do so. Benzodiazepines work by decreasing brain function, and as the dose increases so do the side effects. For example, side effects of benzodiazepines include drowsiness, dizziness, depression, nausea, memory loss, confusion, and blurred vision.

FLUNITRAZEPAM

Flunitrazepam (Rohypnol®) is a benzodiazepine that is not manufactured or legally marketed in the United States, but is smuggled in by traffickers. In the mid-1990s, flunitrazepam was extensively trafficked in Florida and Texas. Known as "rophies," "roofies," and "roach," flunitrazepam gained popularity among younger individuals as a "party" drug. It has also been utilized as a "date rape" drug. In this context, flunitrazepam is placed in the alcoholic drink of an unsuspecting victim to incapacitate them and prevent resistance from sexual assault. The victim is frequently unaware of what has happened to them and often does not report the incident to authorities. A number of actions by the manufacturer of this drug and by government agencies have resulted in reducing the availability and abuse of flunitrazepam in the United States.

LUNESTA

Eszopiclone, known as Lunesta® is a FDA approved nonbenzodiazepine hypnotic used to treat insomnia, primarily with the issue of falling asleep.

GAMMA HYDROXYBUTYRIC ACID (GHB)

In recent years, gamma hydroxybutyric acid (GHB) has emerged as a significant drug of abuse throughout the United States. Abusers of this drug fall into three major groups: (1) users who take GHB for its intoxicant or euphoriant effects; (2) bodybuilders who abuse GHB for its alleged utility as an anabolic agent or as a sleep aid; and (3) individuals who use GHB as a weapon for sexual assault. These categories are not mutually exclusive and an abuser may use the drug illicitly to produce several effects. GHB is frequently taken with alcohol or other drugs that heighten its effects and is often found at bars, nightclubs, rave parties, and gyms. Teenagers and young adults who frequent these establishments are the primary users. Like flunitrazepam, GHB is often referred to as a "date-rape" drug. GHB involvement in rape cases is likely to be unreported or unsubstantiated because GHB is quickly eliminated from the body making detection in body fluids unlikely. Its fast onset of depressant effects may render the victim with little memory of the details of the attack.

GHB produces a wide range of central nervous system effects, including dose-dependent drowsiness, dizziness, nausea, amnesia, visual hallucinations, hypertension, bradycardia, severe respiratory depression, and coma. The use of alcohol in combination with GHB greatly enhances its depressant effects. Overdose frequently requires emergency room care, and many GHB-related fatalities have been reported.

Gamma butyrolactone (GBL) and 1, 4-butanediol are GHB analogues that can be used as substitutes for GHB. When ingested, these analogues are converted to GHB and produce identical effects. GBL is also used in the clandestine production of GHB as an immediate precursor. Both GBL and 1, 4-butanediol have been sold at health food stores and on various internet sites.

The abuse of GHB began to seriously escalate in the mid-1990s. For example, in 1994, there were 55 emergency department episodes involving GHB reported in the Drug Abuse Warning Network (DAWN) system. By 2002, there were 3,330 emergency room episodes. DAWN data also indicated that most users were male, less than 25 years of age, and taking the drug orally for recreational use.

GHB was placed in Schedule I of the CSA in March 2000. Gamma butyrolactone (GBL) was made a List I Chemical in February 2000. GHB has recently been approved as a medication (Xyrem®) for the treatment of cataplexy associated with some types of narcolepsy. This approved medication is in Schedule III of the CSA.

PARALDEHYDE

Paraldehyde (Paral®) is a Schedule IV depressant used most frequently in hospital settings to treat delirium tremens associated with alcohol withdrawal. Many individuals who become addicted to paraldehyde have been initially exposed during treatment for alcoholism and, despite the disagreeable odor and taste, come to prefer it to alcohol. This drug is not used by injection because of tissue damage, and taken orally, it can be irritating to the throat and stomach. One of the signs of paraldehyde use is a strong, characteristic smell to the breath.

CHLORAL HYDRATE

The oldest of the hypnotic (sleep inducing) depressants, chloral hydrate was first synthesized in 1832. Marketed as syrups or soft gelatin capsules, chloral hydrate takes effect in a relatively short time (30 minutes) and will induce sleep in about an hour. A solution of chloral hydrate and alcohol constituted the infamous "knockout drops" or "Mickey Finn." At therapeutic doses, chloral hydrate has little effect on respiration and blood pressure; however, a toxic dose produces severe respiratory depression and very low blood pressure. Chronic use is associated with liver damage and a severe withdrawal syndrome. Although some physicians consider chloral hydrate to be the drug of choice for sedation of children before diagnostic, dental, or medical procedures, its general use as a hypnotic has declined. Chloral hydrate, Noctec®, and other compounds, preparations, or mixtures containing choral hydrate are in Schedule IV of the CSA.

NEWLY MARKETED DRUGS

Zolpidem (Ambien®) and zaleplon (Sonata®) are two relatively new, benzodiazepine-like CNS depressants that have been approved for the short-term treatment of insomnia. Both of these drugs share many of the same properties as the benzodiazepines and are in Schedule IV of the CSA.

VALIUM

Valium, also known as diazepam, is commonly used as a relaxant. It is used for anxiety, muscle spasms, insomnia, alcohol withdrawal, seizures, and other situations. Valium belongs to a bigger group of drugs called benzodiazepines, which are considered to be the most abused pharmaceutical drugs.

XANAX

Xanax, also known as alprazolam, is mainly used to treat anxiety disorders. It belongs to a group of drugs called benzodiazepines, which are relaxants. It has a relatively fast onset, and is considered the most abused of the Benzodiazepines. It has sedative, hypnotic, and muscle relaxant properties.

KAVA KAVA

Kava kava has been used as a ceremonial drink in the Pacific Islands. Its effects on the body are similar to alcohol, providing a relaxing and calming effect. This is used to treat insomnia or anxiety.

The roots of the plant can be ground, ingested and used to make a tea or drink. Because of concerns over severe liver damage, kava should only be used under a doctor's discretion although it is currently available in the U.S. as an over the counter drug.

Alcohol

Alcohol is a depressant that comes from organic sources including grapes, grains and berries. These are fermented or are distilled into a liquid.

Alcohol affects every part of the body. It is carried through the bloodstream to the brain, stomach, internal organs, liver, kidneys, muscles--everywhere. It is absorbed very quickly (as fast as 5-10 minutes) and can stay in the body for several hours.

Alcohol affects the central nervous system and brain. It can make users loosen up, relax, and feel more comfortable or can make them more aggressive.

Unfortunately, it also lowers their inhibitions, which can set them up for dangerous or embarrassing behavior. Alcohol is a drug and is only legal for people over the age 21.

According to the Substance Abuse and Mental Health Services Administration (SAMHSA), 2.6 million young people do not know that a person can die of an overdose of alcohol. Alcohol poisoning occurs when a person drinks a large quantity of alcohol in a short amount of time.

LD50 is a term in toxicology. It refers to the lethal dose of alcohol to the median population, or in other words, what is the lethal dose for 50% of the population. **The LD50 for alcohol is .45% BAC (blood alcohol concentration).**

Erikson's Developmental Stages

Erik Erikson was a psychoanalyst who documented stages of emotional growth in regards to human babies. Each stage has different needs and lessons to be learned. If the child or infant does not learn a specific lesson, he may have a harder time in life down the road. For example, if a baby is crying constantly and is not taken care of, or if they are ignored, they can come to feel mistrust towards others. Another example is found in the young adult stage. The young adult must deal with either being intimate with someone or dealing with feeling isolated. According to Erikson, the most important thing is the development of trust.

Infant   *Trust vs. Mistrust*
Infants gain trust and confidence from their caregivers. If those caregivers are warm and responsive then they will know that the world is good. Mistrust occurs from being handled poorly and inattentiveness on the part of the caregiver.

Toddler   *Autonomy vs. Shame and Doubt*

Children want to make their own decisions. Autonomy is when the parents give the child that necessary free reign over their choices.

Preschooler   *Initiative vs. Guilt*

Children play at different roles. They can try their hand at being a princess or a mother or father to their dolls. Ever wonder why children at this age love dress-up clothes?

School-Age Child   *Industry vs. Inferiority*

Children learn to work with others.

Adolescent   *Identity vs. Role Confusion*

This is the standard teen question: "Who am I?"

Young Adult   *Intimacy vs. Isolation*

Young adults seek emotional ties with others. Because of earlier trust situations (divorce of parents, for example), some young adults are unable to form attachments and this leaves them isolated.

Middle-Age Adult   *Generativity vs. Stagnation*

Generativity means giving to the next generation. Those that do not do these things feel unhappy.

Old Age   *Ego integrity vs. Despair*

In this stage, people think about what they have done with their life. Integrity comes from achieving what one wanted in life. Despair results in fear of death for those that are unhappy with their past.

Jean Piaget

Jean Piaget (1896-1980) was a biologist who originally studied mollusks (publishing twenty scientific papers on them by the time he was 21) but moved into the study of the development of children's understanding, through observing them and talking and listening to them while they worked on exercises he set.

His view of how children's minds work and develop has been enormously influential, particularly in educational theory. His particular insight was the role of maturation (simply growing up) in children's increasing capacity to understand their world: they cannot undertake certain tasks until they are psychologically mature enough to do so.

His research has spawned a great deal more, much of which has undermined the details of his own, but like many other investigators, his importance comes from his overall vision.

He proposed that children's thinking does not develop entirely smoothly; instead, there are certain points at which it 'takes off' and moves into completely new areas and capabilities. He saw these transitions as taking place at about 18 months, 7 years and 11 or 12 years. This has been taken to mean that before these ages children are not capable (no matter how bright) of understanding things in certain ways, and that theory has been used as the basis for scheduling the school curriculum.1 Piaget is a **cognitive theorist.** Piaget believed that the individual actively constructs knowledge about the world.

Piaget's Relevant Definitions

Assimilation: The process by which a person takes material into their mind from the environment, which may mean changing the evidence of their senses to make it fit.

Accommodation: The difference made to one's mind or one's concepts by the process of assimilation. Note that assimilation and accommodation go together; you can't have one without the other.

Classification: The ability to group objects together on the basis of common features.

Class Inclusion: The understanding of more advanced than simple classification, that some classes or sets of objects are also sub-sets of a larger class. (e.g. There is a class of objects called dogs. There is also a class called animals. But all dogs are also animals, so the class of animals includes that of dogs.)

Conservation: The realization that objects or sets of objects stay the same even when they are changed about or made to look different. For example, children can understand that the same amount of liquid is in two differently shaped jars.

Developmental Norm: A statistical measure of typical scores for categories of information.

Egocentrism: The belief that you are the center of the universe and everything revolves around you, and the corresponding inability to see the world as someone else does and adapt to it. Not moral "selfishness", just an early stage of psychological development. The move away from egocentrism is called decentration.

Elaboration: Relating new information to something familiar. An example would be learning how to cook a pasta dish. You may have cooked something similar in the past. In your mind your may think, "This is like that time I made Ramen except now I do…"

Operation: The process of working something out in your head. Young children (in the sensorimotor and pre-operational stages) have to act, and try things out in the real world, to work things out (like count on fingers); older children and adults can do more in their heads, mentally.

Recognition: Is the ability to identify correctly something encountered before.

Recall: Is being able to reproduce knowledge from memory.

Schema (or scheme): The representation in the mind of a set of perceptions, ideas, and/or actions, which go together.

Stage: A period in a child's development in which he or she is capable of understanding some things but not others.

Piaget's Stages of Development

Developmental Stage and Approximate Age	Characteristic Behavior
Sensory Motor Period **(0-24 months)**	
Reflexive Stage (0-2 months)	Simple reflex activity such as grasping and sucking.
Primary Circular Reactions (2-4 months)	Reflexive behaviors occur in stereotyped repetition such as opening and closing fingers repetitively.
Secondary Circular Reactions (4-8 months)	Repetition of actions to reproduce interesting consequences such as kicking one's feet to move a mobile suspended over the crib.
Coordination of Secondary Reactions (8-12 months)	Responses become coordinated into more complex sequences. Actions take on an "intentional" character such as the infant reaches behind a screen to obtain a hidden object.

Tertiary Circular Reactions (12-18 months)	Discovery of new ways to produce the same consequence or obtain the same goal such as the infant pulling a pillow toward him in an attempt to get a toy resting on it.
Invention of New Means Through Mental Combination (18-24 months)	Evidence of an internal representational system. Symbolizing the problem-solving sequence before actually responding. Deferred imitation.

The Preoperational Period (2-7 years)	
Preoperational Phase (2-4 years)	Increased use of verbal representation but speech is egocentric. The beginnings of symbolic rather than simple motor play. Transductive reasoning. Can think about something without the object being present by use of language.
Intuitive Phase (4-7 years)	Speech becomes more social, less egocentric. The child has an intuitive grasp of logical concepts in some areas. However, there is still a tendency to focus attention on one aspect of an object while ignoring others. Concepts formed are crude and irreversible. Easy to believe in magical increase, decrease, disappearance. Reality not firm. Perceptions dominate judgment. In the moralethical realm, the child is not able to show principles underlying best behavior. Rules of a game cannot develop in the mind; only uses simple do's and do not's imposed by authority.

Period of Concrete Operations (7-11 years)
Evidence for organized, logical thought. There is the ability to perform multiple classification tasks, order objects in a logical sequence, and comprehend the principle of conservation. Thinking becomes less transductive and less egocentric. The child is capable of concrete problem solving. Some reversibility now possible (quantities moved can be restored such as in arithmetic: 3+4 = 7 and 7-4 = 3, etc.) Classifying logic-finding bases to sort unlike objects into logical groups where previously it was on superficial perceived attributes such as color. Categorical labels such as "number" or "animal" now available.

Period of Formal Operations (11-15 years)
Thought becomes more abstract, incorporating the principles of formal logic. The ability to generate abstract propositions, multiple hypotheses and their possible outcomes is evident. Thinking becomes less tied to concrete reality. Formal logical systems can be acquired. Can handle proportions, algebraic manipulation, and other purely abstract processes. If $a + b = x$ then $x = a\,b$. If $ma/ca = IQ = 1.00$ then $Ma = CA$. Prepositional logic present, in as-if and ifthen steps. Can use aids such as axioms to transcend human limits on comprehension. Can think hypothetically and test hypothesis. Based on the information in these stages, you can see it is important to have age appropriate materials in school.

Piaget and Freud both agreed that environmental influences could affect the time spent in stages but not the order.

Language Development

Language development begins at about six months. In all areas of the world and cultures, babies start cooing and babbling at six months. This is called pre-speech. The first element of development is the cooing. The second development is babbling. The third is hollow phrases. The fourth is telegraphic speech. Children in early language development are not able to understand figurative language, but they do understand some grammar. One example is the children's books where the main character is told to do a household chore. She is told to "run over these sheets with the iron" and she does just that, holds the iron in her hand and tramples the sheets. To learn more about language development, turn to suffix 1 to read additional information about the stages.

Echolalia is a baby repeating what you just said. At 10-14 months is when most children begin to speak actual words. A professor named Noam Chomsky stated that the ability to develop language skills is inherited in genes. Language theorists believe that a child acquires language through reinforcement from their environment. This would include all people they come in contact with and other things like television.

Telegraphic speech is a speech pattern in which a person eliminates function words from their sentences, instead keeping only the important content words. This is the sort of speech pattern which is typical for children around two years old. The sentences contain a noun and a verb in appropriate and logical order, however they aren't complete sentences. For example, a child would say "go home" instead of "I would like to go home now."

Freud's Psychosexual Stages

Stage	Age	Description
Oral	Birth-1 year	The new ego directs the baby's sucking activities toward breast or bottle. If oral needs are not met appropriately, the individual may develop such habits as thumb sucking, fingernail biting, pencil chewing, overeating and smoking.
Anal	1-3 years	Young toddlers and preschoolers enjoy holding and releasing urine and feces. Toilet training becomes a major issue between parent and child. If parents insist that children be trained before they are ready or make too few demands, conflicts about anal control may appear in the form of extreme orderliness and cleanliness or messiness and disorder.
Phallic	3-6 years	Id impulses transfer to the genitals, and the child finds pleasure in genital stimulation. Freud's Oedipus Conflict for boys and Electra Conflict for girls take place. Young children feel a sexual desire for the other-sex parent. To avoid punishment, they give up this desire and instead adopt the same-sex parent's characteristics and values. As a result, the superego is formed and children feel guilty each time they violate its standards. The relationships between id, ego and superego established at this time determine the individual's basic personality orientation.
Latency	6-11 years	Sexual instincts die down, and the superego develops further. The child acquires new social values from adults outside the family and from play with same-sex peers.
Genital	Adolescence	Puberty causes the sexual impulses of the phallic stage to reappear. If development has been successful during earlier stages, it leads to marriage, mature sexuality, and the birth and rearing of children.

Karen Horney

Karen Horney was born in Germany on September 16, 1885. When she was nine years old, Karen developed a crush on her brother. His rejection of her was the initial cause of the depression that she suffered for the rest of her life. In 1906, Horney entered medical school against her parent's wishes. There she met Oscar Horney, who she married in 1909. She graduated with her medical degree from the University of Berlin in 1913. For a while she studied Freudian theory and explored psychoanalytic theories with Karl Abraham. After four years, she began analyzing patients at the Berlin Psychoanalytic Clinic.

When her husband's business shut down and he developed meningitis, she moved without him to the United States with their three daughters. There she became friends with other notable intellectuals and developed her theories on psychology.
Horney's theory of neurosis is her most prominent theory.

She saw neurosis in a way others did not. Instead of abuse or neglect, Horney named cause of neurosis in adulthood to be parental indifference, which she referred to as the "basic evil." She also saw neurosis as a coping technique and a relatively normal experience. She explained that the needs felt by a neurotic are felt by everybody to some extent, but a neurotic's need for these things is much more intense. A person with neurosis will experience great anxiety if their needs are not met. Horney described ten neuroses, including:

1. the need for acceptance and affection
2. love and intimacy
3. simplicity
4. power
5. the need to manipulate
6. social recognition
7. admiration
8. personal accomplishment
9. independence
10. perfection

She later identified three main coping strategies found within the ten neuroses: compliance (moving towards others) aggression (moving against others) and withdrawal (moving away from others).

Horney also had several Neo-Freudian theories, most of which developed from her disagreement with Freud's theories on female psychology. She rejected his concept of "penis envy" and proposed the concept of "womb envy" in which men feel inferior because they cannot have children. She theorized that men's drive to succeed in the workplace stemmed from this feeling of inferiority.

Horney also did not believe that sex and aggression drive personality. She suggested (instead of Freud's Oedipus complex) that clinging to one parent and jealousy of the other was caused by a disrupted parent-child relationship. Horney's refutation of Freud's theories about women generated more interest in female psychology. Horney also believed that each person has a personal role in their own mental health. In 1942 she published her book "Self-Analysis," in which she discussed the neuroses, psychoanalysis, and how individuals can take advantage of psychoanalytic techniques personally. Horney often encouraged self-analysis and self-help. She believed that, regarding relatively minor neurotic problems, people could be their own psychiatrists.

Defense Mechanisms

Defense mechanisms are developed to help us relieve stress. We can choose to accept, deny or change our perceptions and feelings to be in harmony with our values. Here is a list of the most common defense mechanisms and what they mean:

Denial: Complete rejection of the feeling or situation.

Suppression: Hiding the feelings and not acknowledging them.

Reaction Formation: Turning a feeling into the exact opposite feeling. For example, saying you hate someone you are interested in.

Projection: Projection is transferring your thoughts and feelings onto others. For example, someone who is being unfaithful himself or herself would constantly accuse his or her partner of cheating.

Displacement: Feelings are redirected to someone else. Someone who has a bad day at work and can't complain goes home and yells at their kids instead.

Rationalization: You deny your feelings and come up with ways to justify your behavior.

Regression: Reverting to old behavior to avoid feelings.

Sublimation: A type of displacement, a redirection of the feeling into a socially productive activity.

⌁ *Id, Ego and Super Ego*

Sigmund Freud's analysis of human personality and subconscious drives features three main components id, ego, and superego. Together, these mechanisms combine to aide us in our decision-making and guide us to become the unique individuals that we all are. Robert Young, a professor with expertise in this area, provided the following information used to understand the id, superego and the ego.

The id contains the psychic content related to the primitive instincts of the body, notably sex and aggression, as well as all psychic material that is inherited and present at birth. It functions entirely according to the pleasure-pain principle, its impulses either seeking immediate fulfillment or settling for a compromise fulfillment.

The superego is the ethical component of the personality and provides the moral standards by which the ego operates.

The ego coexists, in psychoanalytic theory; with the id and superego...it is the integrator between the outer and inner worlds, as well as between the id and the superego. The ego gives continuity and consistency to behavior by providing a personal point of reference, which relates the events of the past (retained in memory) and actions of the present and of the future (represented in anticipation and imagination).

The main trio of characters found in Star Trek, the original series -McCoy, Kirk, and Spock -makes for an interesting analogy of human personality as they each show characteristics of Freud's concepts of the id, ego, and superego. Hopefully, this analogy will make it easier for you to understand and remember this theory.

THE ID James T. Kirk, always enjoyed a good fight, risked his ship and crew often, and always fed his libido with an assortment of females. Kirk, with his passion for gratification in terms of aggression and sex, displays characteristics of the id.

THE SUPEREGO Doctor Leonard (Bones) McCoy, always reminded his Captain of the rules and morality of any situation. He also is known for his arguments with Spock, just as the superego and ego are often in conflict.

THE EGO Mr. Spock was the bringer of balance between the impulses of the id and the extreme caution of the superego by his use of logic and understanding of his Captain's needs as well as understanding the morality base of Bones. While Spock and

Bones were often at odds, they always worked toward the same end -a correct and feasible solution to any given situation.

Together Kirk, McCoy, and Spock represent the triadic conflict within all humans, thus the three distinct characters, taken together, form an understanding of the human condition.

Free Association

Free association is a psychoanalytical practice in which the patient is encouraged to share anything that comes to their mind. The method was first used by Sigmund Freud. He believed that an individual's unconscious thoughts would eventually surface naturally. Free association can be achieved as a therapist states a list of words and the patient responds with the first word that comes to their mind. Another application of free association comes as the patient simply describes the path that their thoughts take over a short period of time. The ultimate goal of the therapist is to link the pattern of answers given by a patient to the underlying problem, hidden memories, or repressed emotions.

Maslow's Hierarchy of Needs

Maslow believed that there were five stages of needs that defined how a person behaved and responded in different situations. His theory has been termed Maslow's Hierarchy of Needs, and has been very influential both in its pure form and in the sense that it has influenced many of the theories which followed it.

Maslow's Hierarchy of Needs consists of the following stages, from the top down:

- Self-actualization
- Esteem needs
- Belonging and love
- Safety
- Physical needs

These stages begin at physical needs. An individual first needs to have food, water, and shelter before they can worry about other things. If a person does not have these needs met, then all of their energies will be focused on obtaining them. These are the most basic needs that a person can have filled.

Once those needs are met, an individual may start to think of other needs such as safety. Aside from physical needs which sustain life, safety is the next most important focus of any individual. For example, safety needs may involve purchasing a gun or moving to a more prosperous and safe area.

Once the physical and safety needs are both met (i.e., a person is fed, clothed and safe), Maslow posited that individuals will want to meet needs of belonging and love through relationships. An individual in this third stage of development will seek out relationships with others. This could involve finding friendships with co-workers, entering into a committed relationship, or spending time with family. Any needs related to an individual's social standing with others would fall into this category of needs.

Moving onto the Maslow's fourth stage, esteem needs, once an individual feels loved they may begin to focus on their self-esteem. These needs include how they feel as a person, and what they are contributing to their environments. At this stage, individuals are highly aware of the opinions of those around them, and their actions are motivated by a need to be accepted. For many people, this is the highest stage that they ever reach; however, Maslow argued that the highest stage which a person can attain is selfactualization.

The final stage, self-actualization, describes individuals who are entirely comfortable with themselves, and focused on personal growth and achievement rather than on gaining approval from others.

Maslow believed that a person would progress through these stages chronologically. In other words, he believed that people cannot skip a step. In order to achieve selfactualization, for example, an individual must first satisfy their self-esteem needs.

Classical Conditioning

The first scientific experiment of classical conditioning was done by a Russian scientist named Ivan Pavlov. In Pavlov's famous dog experiment, he would ring a bell and then feed the dogs. Initially, the dogs would salivate when given food. Over time, the dogs began to salivate at the sound of the bell. Classical conditioning describes a link between a stimulus and a response in which a person or animal associates or substitutes a neutral stimulus, such as the bell, with the actual stimulus, the food. Many reflexive reactions, such as a person covering their eyes when something flies in front of their face, or salivating at the smell of their favorite food, can be explained through classical conditioning.

Operant Conditioning

Operant conditioning is a type of conditioning in which a person associates an action with a consequence. The main difference between operant conditioning and classical conditioning is that classical conditioning works more to explain reflexive or unconscious reactions, whereas operant conditioning works to explain elective actions and reactions. For example, a student will wish to do well in school because it brings the consequence of good grades and parental approval. Studies have shown that even infants can be taught certain behaviors using operant conditioning. The name most associated with operant conditioning is B. F. Skinner.

The Premack principle is a system which uses operant conditioning to make less probable actions more likely to occur by using more probable actions as reinforcers. For example, most children do not like doing laundry, making it the less probable action. However, most children do enjoy watching television, making it the more probable action. If a mother tells her children that they can watch television if they do the laundry, she is using the Premack principle, with the television being the reinforcer.

Reinforcers

Operant conditioning depends upon reinforcers as a method of learning. A reinforcer is anything which makes a behavior more likely to reoccur. Reinforcers can be positive or negative. A positive reinforcer is when something pleasant is used to make a behavior more likely. Parents paying their children for good grades or a person giving their pet a treat for doing a trick are both examples of positive reinforcers. A negative reinforcer is when something unpleasant is removed from a situation. For example, if a student studies more, they are less anxious. The anxiety is an unpleasant feeling which is removed as a result of studying, and therefore studying is a form of negative reinforcement. Conditioning can also occur using punishments, which instead of making a behavior more likely to reoccur, attempt to make it less likely to reoccur. Like reinforcers, punishments can be both positive and negative.

In addition to being positive and negative, reinforcers can also be described as extrinsic or intrinsic. An extrinsic reinforcer is something physical (tangible), or from the environment. Payment for work, a treat for doing well, and earning a prize for winning a game are all extrinsic reinforcers. An intrinsic reinforcer, on the other hand, is something which comes from within the individual, or in other words, something emotional. Self-satisfaction or the happiness which comes from praise are intrinsic reinforcers. The values of extrinsic and intrinsic reinforcers are different for everyone.

Learning Theories

John B Watson argued that if psychology was a true science, then psychologists should only study what they could see and measure. Behaviorism, now also called learning theory, is based on the principle of observing and correcting behavior.

A Russian scientist named Ivan Pavlov did a study between stimulus and response. This study most commonly referred to as Pavlov's Dogs, when Pavlov discovered Classical Conditioning.

Pavlov was researching salivation in dogs. He realized that the dogs began to salivate not only at the sight of food but eventually, at the sound of the footsteps of the attendants that were bringing the food. This observation led him through classical conditioning to make a dog salivate when a bell was heard.

Pavlov began by ringing the bell just before feeding the dog and created through several steps salivation by only hearing the sound of the bell. Classical conditioning is when an animal or person responds to a neutral stimulus (like the bell) with a meaningful one (food).

B.F. Skinner was one of the most important learning theorists of our time. Skinner agreed that classical conditioning explains some types of behaviors, but he believed that operant conditioning played a much larger role. Operant conditioning teaches that when a certain action is performed, there are consequences. Operant conditioning reinforces good behavior. You can teach your dog to fetch your slippers by teaching him the action and then giving him a reward. It can be said that all social interactions are a result of operant conditioning, i.e., getting peer approval for your new car or earning a paycheck. Reinforcement is the term for the positive or useful consequence to an action. An intrinsic reinforcer is something that comes from inside the individual, like satisfaction for doing a good job. An extrinsic reinforcer is anything outside yourself, in the environment that reinforces your behavior, such as getting good grades, resulting in a scholarship or discounts on insurance.

Instructional conditioning gives a negative sanction. Extinction is done best gradually through shaping. Extinction is the process of unassociating the condition with the response. When you ring the bell for your cat to get dinner and then don't provide him with any food, gradually the cat will learn not to come when the bell is sounded.

Response extinction is a method of modifying behavior. It ignores the behavior so you don't have the response.

Egocentric behavior means that a child does not take into consideration other people's needs. This is especially important in divorce when the child is in this stage. The child is incapable of understanding that he or she is not the result of the breakup because to that child, the world revolves around them. Children in their preschool years tend to have an egocentric view of the world, in other words thinking centers around the ego or self. This "self-centered" view does not necessarily mean selfish. Egocentric means that the child's perceptions are limited to their own point of view. A child who sees someone crying may bring them their special blanket, assuming that because the blanket makes them happy, it will also make the crying person happy. In this way the child is egocentric, but not selfish.

Social learning theory is the extension of the euphemism actions speak louder than words. If your mother drinks, even though she tells you it is bad and you should not do it, you are likely to become a drinker based on her example.

Modeling is observing someone's, our parents' or our peer's, behavior, and basing our own behavior on it. Explicit role instruction (stereotypes): boys play with trucks and cars, girls wear make-up.

Lewis Terman conducted a longitudinal study of smart kids. The results are that the children are happy adults.

Baby Albert

There once was a boy who was kept in a box. By using classical conditioning, the researchers made the baby afraid of rats. Later because of stimulus generalization, he was afraid of all furry animals. Most children's fears are learned through conditioning. This is a good example of horrendous research ethics.

Stimulus Generalization is when something from conditioning carries over to another related area. You are afraid of spiders; soon you become afraid of all bugs.

Lev Vygotsky developed the theory of social development or social cognition. He stated that every function in the child's cultural development appears twice: first, between people and then inside the child. There were three elements to his theory. First, the idea that social interaction facilitates cognitive improvement. In other words, social learning, or the cultural aspect of a child's life which occurs outside their body, happens before development, which occurs inside the child. The second aspect is the presence of a "More Knowledgeable Other" (MKO). This person is more knowledgeable than the child is in a specific area. It could be a parent, teacher, coach, friend, or even a computer. The third element is the "Zone of Proximal Development" (ZPD). This describes the fact that there is a gap between what the child can do with help, and what they can do on their own. When the child closes the gap, they have learned.

ALBERT BANDURA

The most important theorist involved in self-efficacy theory is Albert Bandura. Bandura claimed that people are primarily motivated by their own perceptions of their ability to do a task well. Self-efficacy, then, is essentially the extent to which a person is confident in their ability. The more self-efficacious a person is, the longer they will work at a task and the more effort they will put into it. According to Bandura, self-efficacy is determined on a basis of four different factors; the four factors are past experiences, the experiences of others, current emotional status, and the feedback received from others.

Although self-efficacy and self-esteem may initially seem to be essentially the same, they are actually distinct measures of how a person perceives themselves. Self-esteem specifically refers to how a person perceives their self-worth. Self-efficacy, on the other hand, is a person's perception of their ability to complete a task. The two measures can coincide, but it is also possible for them to diverge (i.e., a person can have high self-esteem and low self-efficacy and they can alternatively have low self-esteem and high self-efficacy). Although it is important for a person to have a good sense of self-esteem, Bandura argued that self-efficacy was of central importance in an individual's life because it regulates how people spend their time, what things will motivate them, their cognitive and emotional responses to situations, and the work ethic.

To describe how self-efficacy is determined, Bandura proposed a triangular model incorporating three different elements: personal attributes, external factors, and behaviors. Because the development of self-efficacy is a lifelong process, Bandura focused on effectively applying these principles throughout childhood and development (though they are just as relevant in adults). Counseling based on Bandura's theories will focus on these factors when determining what career paths a person would be most suited to.

An example of this theory is an outgoing person will interact with the environment, say a hotel desk clerk, differently than a shy person. The way they interact determines the outcome, possibly a room upgrade which reinforces their outgoing personality, i.e., if I'm funny and outgoing I get extra privileges. A shy person would not have the same reaction because they would not handle the situation the same way. A shy person would not even attempt to do what an outgoing person would do, hence the reaction is different.

Kohlberg's Theory of Moral Development

Level 1: Preconventional morality

Stage 1: Punishment and obedience phase. Whether you will be punished or not determines what is moral or not. For example, you don't speed when driving the car because you know that you might get a ticket, a negative sanction from an authority figure.

Stage 2: A person becomes aware of two different viewpoints. You see the right action as what satisfies your personal needs. You don't speed while driving a car because you want the lower rates on car insurance that you will get having no tickets on your record.

Level 2: Conventional morality

Stage 3: A "good boy-good girl" orientation. You do what is right in order to gain status or approval from other people or society. For example, you don't get speeding tickets while driving because in your circle of friends that would make you appear irresponsible, therefore lowering your social status.

Stage 4: Social-order-maintaining orientation. A person abides by the law because they think that law is a higher order. It is their duty as a responsible citizen to not speed. This type of person would not run a red light in a deserted intersection even if he had been waiting five minutes. They believe that laws cannot be broken under any circumstance.

Level 3: Postconventional morality

Stage 5: The social contract orientation. A person is concerned with how their action might affect society. "I'm not going to speed because I might get into an accident and injure someone."

Stage 6: The universal ethical principle orientation. A person makes decisions according to his or her conscience. Not many, if any, people get to this stage.

Kohlberg believed that you go through these stages one at a time and cannot skip them. According to both Kohlberg and Piaget, the most immature reason to do something is to avoid punishment.

Childhood Issues and Terminology

HURRIED CHILD

For example, one that is always in a hurry, quick to eat, get ready, wash its face.

RESILIENT CHILD

One that bounces back from a difficult situation like abuse.

RITE OF PASSAGE

This is a signal to society that certain rules have changes. This person is no longer a child. Some examples of a rite of passage can include getting a drivers license, having sex for the first time, getting married, etc.

SCHOOL PHOBIA

Dread of school.

CHILDHOOD DEPRESSION

Similar to adult depression usually exhibited as "nobody likes me."

The most direct measure of syntax in middle childhood is the mean link of the utterance (how long their sentences are).

PSYCHOMETRICS

Cultural bias not generally known across all subcultures.

MAINSTREAMING

Putting disabled students with normal students. Children are most likely to achieve if their parents have set high standards and assist the children along the way. Gifted children often hide gifts to fit in.

PSYCHOLOGICAL MALTREATMENT

Not physical abuse but when the child feels rejected or feels failure.

SELF-CONCEPT

Who am I? Self-aware, recognized, defined.

SELF-ESTEEM

Begins in middle childhood.

PEER GROUP

The other students in the environment where children live and attend school.

Stages of friendship:
Momentary playmates, ages 3-7
One way assistance, ages 4-9
Two way, fair weather, ages 6-12 3 Intimate, ages 9-15
4 Autonomous, interdependent, ages 12+

Behavior of a child with a difficult temperament can be managed by patient and consistent parenting. The amount of positive and helpful behavior of school-aged children correlates with the child's history of socialization. If someone wants to develop a secure attachment to a child, they must respond appropriately to their signals like picking up a baby when they cry. A father's role with an infant usually involves more play. Firstborn children are more likely to be motivated to achieve. Sibling rivalry is related to the ages of the children. Most children grow out of it.

INSTITUTIONALIZED CHILDREN

The negative effects of sensory deprivation (not as much attention) are more likely to increase with the length of the stage. Failure to thrive is caused by emotional neglect. They can look healthy but not be thriving. Children are easily stressed concerning divorce, moving and death.

Some health problems that children can get (duration ranging from 1 to 14 days) are measles, whooping cough, mumps, polio, and diphtheria. School exposure can help spread more epidemics and colds. Ninety-percent of all children in kindergarten are immunized.

Deferred imitation is the imitation of a past-observed behavior. A child may see their mother breastfeeding a sibling and may later copy the action with a doll.

Read to children to teach them to read. The Montessori method was created when teachers worked with mentally retarded kids. The teachers gave five-year-olds an Italian national exam and had success. The Montessori method teaches children to realize their full abilities.

Your identity changes as you are socialized (grow up). Family therapy involves the whole family. Some children have emotional disturbances while growing up, including bed-wetting, tics and stuttering. **Gender identity** is the awareness of being a male or female. **Gender conservation** is a child's realization their sex will stay the same.

There are different types of child play. They are in chronological order:

- Unoccupied behavior
- Onlooker
- Solitary independent (plays alone)
- Parallel play (plays around others but not with them)
- Associative
- Cooperative Play

Fear of the dark. For children about six years old, the fear is strong and can appear suddenly. This is what you should do:

- Accept the fear as normal
- Offer reassurance
- Encourage emotions freely

Parenting Styles

Authoritarian: "because I say so" – more prevalent in lower-class families.

Permissive: makes few demands, hardly ever punishes.

Authoritative: Respects individuality, but tries to instill social values.

Death and Bereavement

Many people fear death. In fact, this is the leading of many fears, including fear of public speaking, spiders, heights, confined spaces, etc. There are stages that a person goes through when they find out they have an incurable disease or find out they are going to die. These stages are also known as **Kübler-Ross's Stages of Dying**, which are:

1. Denial (shock) "This could never happen to me. This must be a mistake."
2. Anger (emotion) "This is unfair. Why me?"
3. Bargaining "If you don't die I will do the following…"
4. Preparatory Depression "There's nothing I can do about this."
5. Acceptance "I'm ready."

We each deal with death in "our own way" but go through the same stages which are very similar. Here are the stages:

1. Frozen feelings

2. Emotional release

3. Loneliness

4. Physical symptoms

5. Guilt

6. Panic

7. Hostility

8. Selective memory

9. Struggle for new life pattern

10. A feeling that life is good!

Sample Test Questions

1) What is it called when a person takes material into their mind from the environment?

    A) Assimilation
    B) Accommodation
    C) Classification
    D) Stage
    E) Recall

The correct answer is A:) Assimilation.

2) Which of the following represents that strongest correlation?

    A) -.10
    B) +.23
    C) -.44
    D) +.89
    E) +.55

The correct answer is D:) + .89.

3) Which is NOT a step in the scientific method?

    A) Gather information
    B) Generate hypothesis
    C) Test hypothesis
    D) Revise
    E) None of the above

The correct answer is E:) None of the above.

4) The difference between reality and self-concept is called

    A) Shaping
    B) Behavior rehearsal
    C) Modeling
    D) Incongruence
    E) None of the above

The correct answer is D:) Incongruence.

5) Role playing social situations or behaviors is called

   A) Shaping
   B) Behavior rehearsal
   C) Modeling
   D) Incongruence
   E) None of the above

The correct answer is B:) Behavior rehearsal.

6) What is it called when a person has consistent fear of a serious disease?

   A) Hypochondria
   B) Arachnophobia
   C) Phobia
   D) Obsessive-compulsive disorder
   E) Schizophrenia

The correct answer is A:) Hypochondria.

7) Which of the following created the client-centered theory of psychology?

   A) Alfred Kinsey
   B) Carl Jung
   C) B. F. Skinner
   D) Carl Rogers
   E) Ivan Pavlov

The correct answer is D:) Carl Rogers.

8) What is it called when a person experiences hallucinations and delusions?

   A) Hypochondria
   B) Arachnophobia
   C) Phobia
   D) Obsessive-compulsive disorder
   E) Schizophrenia

The correct answer is E:) Schizophrenia.

9) Which of the following conducted the Baby Monkey experiment?

    A) Harry Harlow
    B) Mary Ainsworth
    C) Sigmund Freud
    D) Jean Piaget
    E) Lawrence Kohlberg

The correct answer is A:) Harry Harlow.

10) Which of the following studied temperament?

    A) Harry Harlow
    B) Mary Ainsworth
    C) Sigmund Freud
    D) Jean Piaget
    E) Lawrence Kohlberg

The correct answer is B:) Mary Ainsworth.

11) Cocaine is which of the following?

    A) Sedative
    B) Narcotic
    C) Stimulant
    D) Hallucinogen
    E) Cannabis

The correct answer is C:) Stimulant.

12) Which of the following became famous for his experiments with dogs and conditioning?

    A) Alfred Kinsey
    B) Carl Jung
    C) B. F. Skinner
    D) Carl Rogers
    E) Ivan Pavlov

The correct answer is E:) Ivan Pavlov.

13) When a person experiences unexpected panic attacks it is called

    A) Bipolar disorder
    B) Panic disorder
    C) Insanity
    D) Agoraphobia
    E) Post-traumatic stress disorder

The correct answer is B:) Panic disorder.

14) When a person has anxiety about panic attacks in social or embarrassing situations?

    A) Bipolar disorder
    B) Panic disorder
    C) Insanity
    D) Agoraphobia
    E) Post-traumatic stress disorder

The correct answer is D:) Agoraphobia.

15) When a person experiences extreme stress with biological and psychological symptoms following a traumatic event it is called

    A) Bipolar disorder
    B) Panic disorder
    C) Insanity
    D) Agoraphobia
    E) Post-traumatic stress disorder

The correct answer is E:) Post-traumatic stress disorder.

16) When you get used to hearing trains pass by and you no longer notice the train it is called

    A) Habituation
    B) Stimulus generalization
    C) Convergence
    D) Conditioning
    E) None of the above

The correct answer is A:) Habituation.

17) Visual sensory memory is called

    A) Iconic memory
    B) Echoic memory
    C) Short-term memory
    D) Chunking
    E) Encoding

The correct answer is A:) Iconic memory.

18) When a person experiences a period with manic and depressive periods it is called

    A) Bipolar disorder
    B) Panic disorder
    C) Insanity
    D) Agoraphobia
    E) Post-traumatic stress disorder

The correct answer is A:) Bipolar disorder.

19) When a person has eating problems, poor body image and maintains low body weight it is called

    A) Anorexia nervosa
    B) Bulimia nervosa
    C) Schizophrenia
    D) Histrionic personality
    E) Somatoform disorder

The correct answer is A:) Anorexia nervosa.

20) LSD is which of the following?

    A) Sedative
    B) Narcotic
    C) Stimulant
    D) Hallucinogen
    E) Cannabis

The correct answer is D:) Hallucinogen.

21) When a person binges on food and then expels the food through regurgitation or diuretics it is called

    A) Anorexia nervosa
    B) Bulimia nervosa
    C) Schizophrenia
    D) Histrionic personality
    E) Somatoform disorder

The correct answer is B:) Bulimia nervosa.

22) _____ is a psychotic disorder.

    A) Anorexia nervosa
    B) Bulimia nervosa
    C) Schizophrenia
    D) Histrionic personality
    E) Somatoform disorder

The correct answer is C:) Schizophrenia.

23) In Maslow's hierarchy of needs if you are in the first stage you are experiencing which need?

    A) Safety
    B) Food
    C) Respect from others
    D) Love
    E) Realized full potential

The correct answer is B:) Food.

24) Codeine is which of the following?

    A) Sedative
    B) Narcotic
    C) Stimulant
    D) Hallucinogen
    E) Cannabis

The correct answer is B:) Narcotic.

25) Alcohol is which of the following?

    A) Sedative
    B) Narcotic
    C) Stimulant
    D) Hallucinogen
    E) Cannabis

The correct answer is A:) Sedative.

26) In Maslow's hierarchy of needs if you are in the fifth stage you are experiencing which need?

    A) Safety
    B) Food
    C) Respect from others
    D) Love
    E) Realized full potential

The correct answer is E:) Realized full potential.

27) Which of the following is NOT one of Kübler-Ross's Stages of Dying?

    A) Denial
    B) Anger
    C) Bargaining
    D) Miracle treatments
    E) Acceptance

The correct answer is D:) Miracle treatments.

28) To study something unobtrusively, which of the following research method should be used?

    A) Case study
    B) Longitudinal study
    C) Survey
    D) Experiment
    E) Naturalistic observation

The correct answer is E:) Naturalistic observation.

29) When a single male legally mates with many different females it is called

    A) Rotation theory
    B) Polygyny
    C) Monogamy
    D) Adaptive
    E) Sexual selection

The correct answer is B:) Polygyny. When the marriage of mating between a man and several women is illegal, it is referred to polygamy.

30) MDMA (Ecstasy), GHB, Rohypnol (Ruffies), Clarity, and Ketamine (Special K) area all examples of what kinds of drugs?

    A) Depressants
    B) Club drugs
    C) Uppers
    D) Prescription drugs
    E) None of the above

The correct answer is B:) Club drugs. Most of these drugs are colorless, flavorless, and odorless. These can be dangerous to non-users as they can be added to beverages undetected.

31) In Maslow's hierarchy of needs if you are in the second stage you are experiencing which need?

    A) Safety
    B) Food
    C) Respect from others
    D) Love
    E) Realized full potential

The correct answer is A:) Safety.

32) When traits are determined by two genes it is called

    A) Monogenic
    B) Polygenic
    C) Polygyny
    D) Heritability
    E) Mutations

The correct answer is B:) Polygenic.

33) What is the school of thought that examines the functions of the mind?

    A) Cognitive
    B) Behavioral
    C) Biological
    D) Psychoanalytical
    E) Humanistic

The correct answer is A:) Cognitive.

34) What is the school of thought that revolves around the individual's unconscious motivation?

    A) Cognitive
    B) Behavioral
    C) Biological
    D) Psychoanalytical
    E) Humanistic

The correct answer is D:) Psychoanalytical.

35) Valium is which of the following?

    A) Sedative
    B) Narcotic
    C) Stimulant
    D) Hallucinogen
    E) Cannabis

The correct answer is A:) Sedative.

36) What is the school of thought that studies and observes behavior?

    A) Cognitive
    B) Behavioral
    C) Biological
    D) Psychoanalytical
    E) Humanistic

The correct answer is B:) Behavioral.

37) Which area of the brain is related to hearing?

    A) Occipital lobe
    B) Temporal lobe
    C) Frontal lobe
    D) Parietal lobe
    E) Cerebral cortex

The correct answer is B:) Temporal lobe.

38) Which area of the brain is related to intelligence?

    A) Occipital lobe
    B) Temporal lobe
    C) Frontal lobe
    D) Parietal lobe
    E) Cerebral cortex

The correct answer is C:) Frontal lobe.

39) This part of the eye protects and manages its shape?

    A) Sclera
    B) Iris
    C) Pupil
    D) Cornea
    E) Lens

The correct answer is A:) Sclera.

40) _____ is a clear membrane in front of the eye.

    A) Sclera
    B) Iris
    C) Pupil
    D) Cornea
    E) Lens

The correct answer is D:) Cornea.

41) _____ is a ring of muscles that make up the colored part of the eye.

    A) Sclera
    B) Iris
    C) Pupil
    D) Cornea
    E) Lens

The correct answer is B:) Iris.

42) The part of the eye that looks black and is the opening of the iris is called

    A) Sclera
    B) Iris
    C) Pupil
    D) Cornea
    E) Lens

The correct answer is C:) Pupil.

43) The _____ is at the back of the eye and is light sensitive.

    A) Sclera
    B) Iris
    C) Pupil
    D) Cornea
    E) Retina

The correct answer is E:) Retina.

44) Circadian rhythms complete

    A) Every 24 hours
    B) Every day
    C) Every 28 days
    D) Less than 24 hours
    E) None of the above

The correct answer is A:) Every 24 hours.

45) Infradian rhythms complete

    A) Every 24 hours
    B) Longer than 24 hours
    C) Every 28 days
    D) Less than 24 hours
    E) None of the above

The correct answer is B:) Longer than 24 hours.

46) Which of the following is NOT one of the six primary emotions?

    A) Sadness
    B) Happiness
    C) Fear
    D) Surprise
    E) Anxiety

The correct answer is E:) Anxiety.

47) Which area is the largest part of the brain?

    A) Occipital lobe
    B) Temporal lobe
    C) Frontal lobe
    D) Hypothalamus
    E) Cerebral cortex

The correct answer is E:) Cerebral cortex.

48) If you need to study the long-term effects of smoking which of the following would you use?

    A) Case study
    B) Longitudinal study
    C) Survey
    D) Experiment
    E) Naturalistic observation

The correct answer is B:) Longitudinal study.

49) Which area of the brain is related to vision?

    A) Occipital lobe
    B) Temporal lobe
    C) Frontal lobe
    D) Parietal lobe
    E) Cerebral cortex

The correct answer is A:) Occipital lobe.

50) _____ is also known as borderline personality disorder.

    A) Anorexia nervosa
    B) Bulimia nervosa
    C) Schizophrenia
    D) Histrionic personality
    E) Somatoform disorder

The correct answer is D:) Histrionic personality.

51) Which part of the brain is responsible for storing memories?

    A) Occipital lobe
    B) Temporal lobe
    C) Hippocampus
    D) Parietal lobe
    E) Cerebral cortex

The correct answer is C:) Hippocampus.

52) When a person experiences real biological symptoms that cannot be explained by any medical means it is called

    A) Anorexia nervosa
    B) Bulimia nervosa
    C) Schizophrenia
    D) Histrionic personality
    E) Somatoform disorder

The correct answer is E:) Somatoform disorder.

53) Which of the following are narcotics?

A) Peyote
B) Codeine
C) LSD
D) Advil
E) None of the above

The correct answer is B:) Codeine. Codeine is a narcotic, which is any drug derived from opium.

54) Women's menstrual cycles complete

A) Every 24 hours
B) Every day
C) Every 28 days
D) Less than 24 hours
E) None of the above

The correct answer is C:) Every 28 days.

55) Marijuana is which of the following?

A) Sedative
B) Narcotic
C) Stimulant
D) Hallucinogen
E) Cannabis

The correct answer is E:) Cannabis.

56) In Maslow's hierarchy of needs if you are in the third stage you are experiencing which need?

A) Safety
B) Food
C) Respect from others
D) Love
E) Realized full potential

The correct answer is D:) Love.

57) In Maslow's hierarchy of needs if you are in the fourth stage you are experiencing which need?

    A) Safety
    B) Food
    C) Respect from others
    D) Love
    E) Realized full potential

The correct answer is C:) Respect from others.

58) Which of the following measures muscle activity?

    A) Electroencephalographs
    B) Electromyographs
    C) Electrooculographs
    D) Electrocardiographs
    E) None of the above

The correct answer is B:) Electromyographs.

59) Heroin is which of the following?

    A) Sedative
    B) Narcotic
    C) Stimulant
    D) Hallucinogen
    E) Cannabis

The correct answer is B:) Narcotic.

60) Which of the following measures heart activity?

    A) Electroencephalographs
    B) Electromyographs
    C) Electrooculographs
    D) Electrocardiographs
    E) None of the above

The correct answer is D:) Electrocardiographs.

61) Which type of conditioning reinforces good behavior?

    A) Operant conditioning
    B) Extinction
    C) Classical conditioning
    D) Aversion therapy
    E) None of the above

The correct answer is A:) Operant conditioning.

62) What is the process of removing the condition with the response?

    A) Operant conditioning
    B) Extinction
    C) Classical conditioning
    D) Aversion therapy
    E) None of the above

The correct answer is B:) Extinction.

63) Auditory sensory memory is called

    A) Iconic memory
    B) Echoic memory
    C) Short-term memory
    D) Chunking
    E) Encoding

The correct answer is C:) Short-term memory.

64) Which area of the brain is related to body sensations?

    A) Occipital lobe
    B) Temporal lobe
    C) Frontal lobe
    D) Parietal lobe
    E) Cerebral cortex

The correct answer is D:) Parietal lobe.

65) When information is processed it is called

    A) Iconic memory
    B) Echoic memory
    C) Short-term memory
    D) Chunking
    E) Encoding

The correct answer is E:) Encoding.

66) When you have one or more pauses in breathing or shallow breaths while you sleep it is called sleep _____.

    A) Walking
    B) Talking
    C) Snoring
    D) Apnea
    E) Encoding

The correct answer is D:) Apnea.

67) What is the difference made to one's mind by the process of assimilation?

    A) Assimilation
    B) Accommodation
    C) Classification
    D) Stage
    E) Recall

The correct answer is B:) Accommodation.

68) Which of the following is a stimulant?

    A) Cocaine
    B) Beer
    C) Wine
    D) Cannabis
    E) None of the above

The correct answer is A:) Cocaine.

69) The _____ system houses the structures for memory and emotion.

    A) Occipital
    B) Temporal
    C) Hippocampus
    D) Limbic
    E) Cerebral

The correct answer is D:) Limbic.

70) What is the ability to group objects together on the basis of common features?

    A) Assimilation
    B) Accommodation
    C) Classification
    D) Stage
    E) Recall

The correct answer is C:) Classification.

71) What is a period in a child's development in which he or she is capable of understanding some things but not others?

    A) Assimilation
    B) Accommodation
    C) Classification
    D) Stage
    E) Recall

The correct answer is D:) Stage.

72) What is the process of working something out in your head?

    A) Egocentrism
    B) Elaboration
    C) Operation
    D) Recognition
    E) Conservation

The correct answer is C:) Operation.

73) Which of the following was a psychoanalyst?

    A) Harry Harlow
    B) Mary Ainsworth
    C) Sigmund Freud
    D) Jean Piaget
    E) Lawrence Kohlberg

The correct answer is C:) Sigmund Freud.

74) What is it called when you are able to reproduce knowledge from memory?

    A) Assimilation
    B) Accommodation
    C) Classification
    D) Stage
    E) Recall

The correct answer is E:) Recall.

75) Which of the following created the pre-operational period?

    A) Harry Harlow
    B) Mary Ainsworth
    C) Sigmund Freud
    D) Jean Piaget
    E) Lawrence Kohlberg

The correct answer is D:) Jean Piaget.

76) What is the ability to identify correctly something encountered before?

    A) Egocentrism
    B) Elaboration
    C) Operation
    D) Recognition
    E) Conservation

The correct answer is D:) Recognition.

77) What is the realization that objects or sets of objects stay the same even when they are changes about or made to look different?

    A) Egocentrism
    B) Elaboration
    C) Operation
    D) Recognition
    E) Conservation

The correct answer is E:) Conservation.

78) Which of the following measures brain waves?

    A) Electroencephalographs
    B) Electromyographs
    C) Electrooculographs
    D) Electrocardiographs
    E) None of the above

The correct answer is A:) Electroencephalographs.

79) Which is a surgical procedure which removes the nerve tracts in the frontal lobes?

    A) Chemical castration
    B) Effort effect
    C) MRI
    D) Lobotomy
    E) None of the above

The correct answer is D:) Lobotomy.

80) Which of the following measures eye movement?

    A) Electroencephalographs
    B) Electromyographs
    C) Electrooculographs
    D) Electrocardiographs
    E) None of the above

The correct answer is C:) Electrooculographs.

81) Which of the following created the Theory of Moral Development?

    A) Harry Harlow
    B) Mary Ainsworth
    C) Sigmund Freud
    D) Jean Piaget
    E) Lawrence Kohlberg

The correct answer is E:) Lawrence Kohlberg.

82) Which of the following was an associate of Freud but believed that social motives effected choices more than sexual urges?

    A) Alfred Adler
    B) Albert Bandura
    C) Alfred Binet
    D) Abraham Maslow
    E) Lewis Terman

The correct answer is A:) Alfred Adler.

83) Which of the following is an amphetamine?

    A) Caffeine
    B) Advil
    C) Wine
    D) LSD
    E) None of the above

The correct answer is A:) Caffeine. Caffeine is an amphetamine. It is a stimulant to the central nervous system.

84) Trust vs. Mistrust is Erikson's developmental stage which occurs while a

    A) Infant
    B) Toddler
    C) Preschooler
    D) School-age child
    E) Adolescent

The correct answer is A:) Infant.

85) _____ is the earliest sound a child makes to communicate?

    A) Babbling
    B) Cooing
    C) Echolalia
    D) Crying
    E) None of the above

The correct answer is D:) Crying.

86) Which defense mechanism occurs when someone hides their feelings and does not acknowledge them?

    A) Denial
    B) Suppression
    C) Reaction formation
    D) Projection
    E) Displacement

The correct answer is B:) Suppression.

87) What type of research is conducted by watching the subject?

    A) Naturalistic observation
    B) Longitudinal research
    C) Conditioning
    D) Operant conditioning
    E) Extinction

The correct answer is A:) Naturalistic observation.

88) Which of the following created the Stanford-Binet Intelligence Scale?

    A) Alfred Adler
    B) Albert Bandura
    C) Alfred Binet
    D) Abraham Maslow
    E) Lewis Terman

The correct answer is E:) Lewis Terman.

89) When a child learns something from watching another person perform this task it is called

    A) Shaping
    B) Behavior rehearsal
    C) Modeling
    D) Incongruence
    E) None of the above

The correct answer is C:) Modeling.

90) Which of the following is NOT a monocular cue?

    A) Size
    B) Texture
    C) Overlap
    D) Linear perspective
    E) Double vision

The correct answer is E:) Double vision.

91) Which of the following created the Theory of Needs?

    A) Alfred Adler
    B) Albert Bandura
    C) Alfred Binet
    D) Abraham Maslow
    E) Lewis Terman

The correct answer is D:) Abraham Maslow.

92) Combining small pieces of information into bigger pieces of information is called

    A) Iconic memory
    B) Echoic memory
    C) Short-term memory
    D) Chunking
    E) Encoding

The correct answer is D:) Chunking.

93) A sedative drug will

    A) Decrease heart rate
    B) Increase heart rate
    C) Improve eye sight
    D) Increase endorphins
    E) None of the above

The correct answer is A:) Decrease heart rate. Sedatives produce a relaxing effect, but not sleep.

94) Which of the following believed in a collective unconscious that holds universal human memories?

    A) Alfred Kinsey
    B) Carl Jung
    C) B. F. Skinner
    D) Carl Rogers
    E) Ivan Pavlov

The correct answer is B:) Carl Jung.

95) Which of the following conducted the famous Bobo doll study, showing that children do not need negative nor positive reinforcement to learn?

    A) Alfred Adler
    B) Albert Bandura
    C) Alfred Binet
    D) Abraham Maslow
    E) Lewis Terman

The correct answer is B:) Albert Bandura.

96) Ultradian rhythms complete

    A) Every 24 hours
    B) Every day
    C) Every 28 days
    D) More than once per day
    E) None of the above

The correct answer is D:) More than once per day.

97) Which of the following statements is the best example of telegraphic speech?

    A) My oldest and prettiest sister will visit with us next week
    B) My sister will visit next week
    C) Sister visit week
    D) My sister will be coming to visit me next week for three days
    E) None of the above

The correct answer is C:) Sister visit week. Telegraphic speech is a speech pattern which eliminates function words, and keeps only the content words of a sentence.

98) Which of the following created the Binet-Simon scale which was later revised into an intelligence test?

    A) Alfred Adler
    B) Albert Bandura
    C) Alfred Binet
    D) Abraham Maslow
    E) Lewis Terman

The correct answer is C:) Alfred Binet.

99) Which of the following was a leading sex researcher?

    A) Alfred Kinsey
    B) Carl Jung
    C) B. F. Skinner
    D) Carl Rogers
    E) Ivan Pavlov

The correct answer is A:) Alfred Kinsey.

100) What is the school of thought that believes all people are inherently good?

    A) Cognitive
    B) Behavioral
    C) Biological
    D) Psychoanalytical
    E) Humanistic

The correct answer is E:) Humanistic.

101) Which of the following correctly shows the personality types represented by the acronym OCEAN?

    A) Affectionate, conscientiousness, extroversion, neuroticism, and openness
    B) Extroversion, neuroticism, friendliness, openness, and kindness
    C) Conscientiousness, extroversion, agreeableness, neuroticism, and openness
    D) Openness, niceness, conscientiousness, extroversion, and agreeableness
    E) None of the above

The correct answer is C:) Conscientiousness, extroversion, agreeableness, neuroticism, and openness. OCEAN refers to the Big Five personality types.

102) Another name for working memory is

    A) Iconic memory
    B) Echoic memory
    C) Short-term memory
    D) Chunking
    E) Encoding

The correct answer is C:) Short-term memory.

103) What is the school of thought that believes the behavior and personality are linked to genes?

    A) Cognitive
    B) Behavioral
    C) Biological
    D) Psychoanalytical
    E) Humanistic

The correct answer is C:) Biological.

104) Agreeableness is one of the big five personality types. Which of the following is NOT a characteristic of agreeableness?

A) Friendly
B) Sensitive
C) Compassionate
D) None of the above
E) All of the above

The correct answer is B:) Sensitive. Agreeableness describes a person who is trusting, altruistic, kind, affectionate, compassionate, and cooperative. Sensitivity is a characteristic of neuroticism.

105) Which of the following studied operant conditioning?

A) Alfred Kinsey
B) Carl Jung
C) B. F. Skinner
D) Carl Rogers
E) Sigmund Freud

The correct answer is C:) B. F. Skinner.

106) When a person has a fear of spiders it is called

A) Obsessive-compulsive disorder
B) Depression
C) Arachnophobia
D) Claustrophobia
E) Mania

The correct answer is C:) Arachnophobia.

107) Another word for average

A) Mode
B) Median
C) Mean
D) Standard deviation
E) None of the above

The correct answer is C:) Mean.

108) A person who does not enjoy the activities they used to. They also experience a range of other symptoms include lethargy. They are suffering from

    A) Obsessive-compulsive disorder
    B) Depression
    C) Arachnophobia
    D) Claustrophobia
    E) Mania

The correct answer is B:) Depression.

109) What is it called when a person has a fear of enclosed spaces, such as elevators?

    A) Obsessive-compulsive disorder
    B) Depression
    C) Arachnophobia
    D) Claustrophobia
    E) Mania

The correct answer is D:) Claustrophobia.

110) In _____ therapy, a negative behavior is reinforced by a shock.

    A) Aversion
    B) Client-centered
    C) Psychoanalytical
    D) Group
    E) None of the above

The correct answer is A:) Aversion.

111) When a patient starts with small steps to overcome a difficult obstacle it is called

    A) Shaping
    B) Behavior rehearsal
    C) Modeling
    D) Incongruence
    E) None of the above

The correct answer is A:) Shaping.

112) Anosmia is the loss of

    A) Sight
    B) Hearing
    C) Smell
    D) Touch
    E) Both B and C

The correct answer is C:) Smell. Anosmia is the partial or complete loss of smell. Partial anosmia is common with sinus infections or colds, but it can also become permanent with other problems such as old age.

113) What is the belief that you are the center of the universe?

    A) Egocentrism
    B) Elaboration
    C) Operation
    D) Recognition
    E) Conservation

The correct answer is A:) Egocentrism.

114) Sleep walking occurs in what stage of sleep?

    A) Stage 1
    B) Stage 2
    C) Stage 3
    D) Stage 4
    E) Stage 5

The correct answer is D:) Stage 4.

115) The Big Five personality types are assessed through a test. People with similar scores

    A) Tend to work well together
    B) Should not work together
    C) Do not balance each other out
    D) Two of the above
    E) None of the above

The correct answer is A:) Tend to work well together. People with similar scores usually have similar work attitudes, similar problem solving methods, and respond well to each other's demeanor.

116) The ability of an individual to tie their shoes with little conscious thought is a result of which type of memory?

    A) Procedural memory
    B) Explicit memory
    C) Sensory memory
    D) Long-term memory
    E) Episodic memory

The correct answer is A:) Procedural memory. Procedural memory is also known as implicit memory. These are memories that are specifically related to performing certain actions (or procedures) that become almost automatic due to frequent repetition. Over time these actions essentially become automatic because they have been stored in this portion of long-term memory.

117) A person routinely turns the light on and off several times. They are suffering from

    A) Obsessive-compulsive disorder
    B) Depression
    C) Arachnophobia
    D) Claustrophobia
    E) Mania

The correct answer is A:) Obsessive-compulsive disorder.

118) It typically takes about how many minutes to reach REM sleep?

    A) 5
    B) 20
    C) 30
    D) 60
    E) 90

The correct answer is E:) 90. It typically takes 90 minutes to reach REM sleep.

119) If an individual believes that their actions control what happens in their lives they have a(n)

A) External locus of control
B) Learned helplessness
C) Internal locus of control
D) Situational attribution
E) Intrinsic attribution

The correct answer is C:) Internal locus of control. Locus of control is used to describe the scope of control an individual feels they have in their environment. An internal locus indicates that a person feels that they have control. An external locus indicates that an individual feels that their environment is controlled by factors outside their control.

120) A family moves to the United States from Mexico. With time, they begin to take on elements of American culture; however, they strive to retain some elements of their Mexican culture as well. This describes

A) Assimilation
B) Cultural pluralism
C) Acculturation
D) Racial discrimination
E) None of the above

The correct answer is C:) Acculturation. Assimilation, on the other hand, would involve the initial culture being supplanted by the new culture.

121) According to Erikson's developmental stages, what basic conflict is associated with the early childhood stage?

A) Autonomy vs. Shame and Doubt
B) Trust vs. Mistrust
C) Initiative vs. Guilt
D) Industry vs. Interiority
E) None of the above

The correct answer is A:) Autonomy vs. Shame and Doubt. During early childhood, children experience the autonomy vs. shame and doubt conflict while they potty train.

122) The tendency to seek balance and normalcy is called

A) Centrality
B) Helplessness
C) Dialectics
D) Homeostasis
E) Attribution

The correct answer is D:) Homeostasis. Homeostasis is also called equilibrium. The human body will naturally seek to maintain balance. Imbalance is a sign that something is wrong. For example, a fever is a lack of homeostasis in temperature and signals sickness.

123) Which of the following does NOT describe a problem of test validity?

A) It does not adequately demonstrate differences between individuals or circumstances.
B) It does not give a consistent or standard score between individuals or different takings.
C) It does not accurately test the information that it is meant to.
D) All of the above describe problems with test validity.
E) None of the above

The correct answer is B:) It does not give a consistent or standard score between individuals or different takings. This describes a problem of test reliability, not test validity.

124) Eating or sleep disorders are classified in which axis of the DSM-IV?

A) Axis I
B) Axis II
C) Axis III
D) Axis IV
E) None of the above

The correct answer is A:) Axis I. Axis I includes clinical disorders usually diagnosed in infancy, childhood, or adolescence.

125) According to Karen Horney, neurosis is

    A) A coping technique
    B) Caused by abuse and neglect in childhood
    C) An uncommon occurrence
    D) All of the above
    E) None of the above

The correct answer is A:) A coping technique. Horney saw neurosis as an attempt to make life bearable.

126) The first IQ test was the

    A) Simon-Binet scale
    B) RIASEC
    C) Rorschach Inkblot Test
    D) DSM-IV
    E) None of the above

The correct answer is A:) Simon-Binet scale. The test was meant to be used in schools to determine which children should be placed in special classrooms for mental retardation.

127) Galvanic skin response is measured for use in

    A) Autoimmune tests
    B) Polygraph tests
    C) Frequency exams
    D) Association tests
    E) Rooting reflex tests

The correct answer is B:) Polygraph tests. The tests work because when a person becomes anxious or angry or aroused the autonomic nervous system automatically responds with changes in blood pressure or temperature. These changes are measurable through the skin and can be powerful signs that a person is lying.

128) Which of the following is not a regulation for animal research studies?

    A) Humane living conditions
    B) Least amount of suffering
    C) Regularly inspecting housing areas
    D) Obtained legally
    E) All of the above are regulations involved in animal research studies

The correct answer is E:) All of the above are regulations involved in animal research studies. The use of animal research in psychological studies in invaluable. To protect animals from possible abuse, the APA established guidelines ensuring their humane treatment.

129) Free association is based on the theory that

    A) A person's unconscious thoughts will eventually surface
    B) Individuals have no control over their conscious thought
    C) Unconscious behaviors will never manifest consciously
    D) Thoughts of freedom tend to associate with happiness
    E) None of the above

The correct answer is A:) A person's unconscious thoughts will eventually surface. This is a pattern developed by Freud to replace hypnosis in treatment. The ultimate goal of the therapist is to link the pattern of answers given by a patient to the underlying problem, hidden memories, or repressed emotions.

130) When was the first psychology lab established?

    A) 1517
    B) 1776
    C) 1810
    D) 1879
    E) 1961

The correct answer is D:) 1879. The world's first psychology lab is credited to Wilhelm Wundt in Germany. The lab was established in 1879 and was an academic lab devoted to the study of psychology.

131) Newborns reflexively turn their heads and open their mouths when their cheeks) are touched. This is referred to as the

    A) Grasp reflex
    B) Rooting reflex
    C) Parachute reflex
    D) Tonic reflex
    E) Startle reflex

The correct answer is B:) Rooting reflex. The purpose of this reflex is to encourage successful breastfeeding in newborns. When their cheek is stroked they will turn in that direction and begin a sucking motion.

132) Which of the following correctly pairs a dependent and an independent variable?

    A) Independent: Temperature, Dependent: Cooking time
    B) Dependent: Study time, Independent: Test score
    C) Independent: Number of friends, Dependent: Social skills
    D) Dependent: Number of chickens, Independent: Eggs laid
    E) Independent: Calories burned, Dependent: Distance run

The correct answer is A:) Independent: Temperature, Dependent: Cooking time. Independent variables are the aspects of a situation which effect or determine the measure of other variables. In the example, the amount of time it takes for something to cook will depend on the temperature it is cooking at. In each of the other four examples, the dependent and independent variables have been swapped.

133) What links the two sides of the brain?

    A) Brain stem
    B) Cerebral cortex
    C) Frontal lobe
    D) Corpus callosum
    E) Motor cortex

The correct answer is D:) Corpus callosum. The corpus callosum is the highest content of white matter in the brain. It is structured to transmit impulses from one side of the brain to the other as fast as possible.

134) Which type of therapy is most likely to use token economies?

    A) Operant conditioning
    B) Free association
    C) Classical conditioning
    D) Cognitive dissonance
    E) Situational conditioning

The correct answer is A:) Operant conditioning. Operant conditioning based on principles of rewards and consequences for actions. Token economies use tokens as a form of reward which makes the two theories work well together.

135) A person who views their own culture as superior to all others is said to be

    A) Acculturated
    B) Egocentric
    C) Stereotypical
    D) Ethnocentric
    E) None of the above

The correct answer is D:) Ethnocentric. A person with an ethnocentric mindset will often view their own culture as dominant and then rank all others in relation to it. Ethnocentricity will often lead to stereotyping and racism.

136) Which of the following describes cognitive dissonance theory?

    A) It is natural for the mind to allow some confusion to exist, and it will not seek answers to troubling or frightening questions.
    B) When individuals experience contradicting situations they will seek to achieve consistency in their minds by changing attitudes or beliefs about the situations.
    C) Different individuals are able to view situations in different ways. Often men and women have different cognitive functions that lead them to different conclusions.
    D) There is a tendency for the mind to search for contradicting opinions. Contractions bring stability and consistency of thought.
    E) None of the above

The correct answer is B:) When individuals experience contradicting situations they will seek to achieve consistency in their minds by changing attitudes or beliefs about the situations. Cognitive dissonance is based on the fact that all people experience contradictions at some point. The brain will naturally seek to reconcile them, which means either new information must come forward, or a belief must change.

137) If you believe that a person makes a choice because "that's just the way that they are" it is an example of

    A) Dispositional attribution
    B) Situational attribution
    C) Extrinsic attribution
    D) Collective attribution
    E) Intrinsic attribution

The correct answer is A:) Dispositional attribution. Dispositional attribution is the theory that an individual's choices are derived from within themselves. This viewpoint claims that an individual's choices are made internally based on personality. In contrast, situational attribution is the viewpoint that choices are reflective of situations.

138) Which of the following is most likely to be an intrinsic motivator?

    A) Cleaning the house out of a desire for praise
    B) Studying before a test to get a good grade
    C) Working overtime for more money
    D) Running a marathon to get a trophy
    E) Doing a puzzle for the sense of accomplishment

The correct answer is E:) Doing a puzzle for the sense of accomplishment. Intrinsic motivators are motivations that come from within an individual. Praise, happiness, and contentment are all powerful forces that motivate people to act. Extrinsic motivators are typically in the form of rewards and punishments.

139) Learned helplessness occurs when

    A) An individual is repeatedly exposed to rewards and loses desire to make their own decisions
    B) An individual is repeatedly told that they are helpless and they begin to believe it
    C) An individual is repeatedly given opportunities to change their situation but don't
    D) An individual is repeatedly deprived of necessities of life and loses will to live
    E) An individual is repeatedly subjected to an adverse stimulus over which they have no control

The correct answer is E:) An individual is repeatedly subjected to an adverse stimulus over which they have no control. This creates a feeling in the subject that they have no control over their situation and they stop trying to avoid the stimulus.

140) What is the process of relating new information to something familiar?

    A) Egocentrism
    B) Elaboration
    C) Operation
    D) Recognition
    E) Conservation

The correct answer is B:) Elaboration.

141) Which of the following drugs is approved by the FDA to treat insomnia?

    A) Xanax
    B) Lunesta
    C) Claratin
    D) Mescaline
    E) None of the above

The correct answer is B:) Lunesta. Lunesta is approved by the FDA to treat insomnia.

142) Which of the following is NOT a category of long-term memory?

    A) Procedural memory
    B) Declarative memory
    C) Implicit memory
    D) Sensory memory
    E) Explicit memory

The correct answer is D:) Sensory memory. Sensory memory has the shortest span, typically less than one second, and processes the greatest amount of information. It holds the record of all events relating to the five senses. If information isn't immediately important, it is typically forgotten instantly.

143) An aptitude test may be used to

    A) Screen employees for job positions
    B) Test the fitness of an individual
    C) Help determine what jobs would be best for a person
    D) Both A and C
    E) None of the above

The correct answer is D:) Both A and C. They can be based on anything from numeric abilities, abstract reasoning, mechanical knowledge or any other information considered important to the employer.

144) A dog that bypasses its food bowl and goes straight to its master is considered to be at the _____ level of Maslow's Hierarchy of Needs.

A) Self-actualization
B) Esteem needs
C) Belongingness and love needs
D) Safety needs
E) Physiological needs

The correct answer is C:) Belongingness and love needs. At this level in Maslow's Hierarchy of Needs, a dog/person seeks intimate relationships or the need for social interactions.

145) Justification of _____, trained personnel, proper caring and housing of animal subjects, lawful animal acquisition, and documentation of experimental procedures are just a few of the specific requirements that must be satisfied when using animals for psychological experiments.

A) Existence
B) Research
C) Documentation
D) File-sharing
E) None of the above

The correct answer is B:) Research. The American Psychological Association has provided strict guidelines that must be adhered to when using animal subjects.

146) By boosting _____ and serotonin, the ADHD drug Ritalin can help a person concentrate more fully on a given task or activity.

A) Histamine
B) Norepinephrine
C) Dopamine
D) Epinephrine
E) None of the above

The correct answer is C:) Dopamine. The other options are also monoamine neurotransmitters, but do not have the same interaction with Ritalin.

147) Light waves travel as _____ waves, which can travel through a vacuum. Sound waves are known to travel as _____ waves, which cannot travel through a vacuum.

A) Latitudinal, longitudinal
B) Longitudinal, transverse
C) Transverse, longitudinal
D) Longitudinal, latitudinal
E) None of the above

The correct answer is C:) Transverse, longitudinal. The other answers are variations on the correct answer.

148) _____ is a tactic used to get someone to agree to a larger request after they agree to a more reasonable request first.

A) Toe-in-the-door technique
B) Finger-in-the-door technique
C) Neck-in-the-door technique
D) Arm-in-the-door technique
E) Foot-in-the-door technique

The correct answer is E:) Foot-in-the-door technique.

149) A _____ is any agent that can cause disruption in the development of an embryo or fetus.

A) Dodecatogen
B) Teratogen
C) Decatogen
D) Tetratogen
E) Hexatogen

The correct answer is B:) Teratogen. Teratogens can be classified as a drug, chemical, infection, or even radiation.

150) The central nervous system (CNS) is composed of the _____ and the _____.

    A) Brain, spinal cord
    B) Brain, skeletal structure
    C) Spinal cord, muscle structure
    D) Spinal cord, pituitary gland
    E) None of the above

The correct answer is A:) Brain, spinal cord. The CNS is part of the nervous system as a whole and contains the brain and spinal cord. The peripheral nervous system is also part of the nervous system as a whole and is composed of myelinated sensory and motor neurons that level the CNS.

151) _____ processing refers to your brain processing information as it comes in, while _____ processing is your brain's application of knowledge and what it perceives to fill in the blanks.

    A) Top-down, bottom-up
    B) Top-down, sideways
    C) Bottom-up, sideways
    D) Bottom-up, top-down
    E) Sideways, bottom-up

The correct answer is D:) Bottom-up, top-down.

152) During the _____ stage of sleep, more than 50% of the waves seen on an EEG graph are delta waves.

    A) First
    B) Second
    C) Third
    D) Fourth
    E) REM

The correct answer is D:) Fourth. The third and fourth stage both produce delta waves since this is when we are in delta sleep, but stage four produces more than 50% of the delta waves, meaning we are in a deep sleep.

153) The _____ of light signifies the intensity of a light relative to similar light wavelengths.

A) Attitude
B) Amplitude
C) Latitude
D) Longitude
E) None of the above

The correct answer is B:) Amplitude. The other answers are variations on the correct answer.

Test Taking Strategies

Here are some test-taking strategies that are specific to this test and to other CLEP tests in general:

- Keep your eyes on the time. Pay attention to how much time you have left.

- Read the entire question and read all the answers. Many questions are not as hard to answer as they may seem. Sometimes, a difficult sounding question really only is asking you how to read an accompanying chart. Chart and graph questions are on most CLEP tests and should be an easy free point.

- If you don't know the answer immediately, the new computer-based testing lets you mark questions and come back to them later if you have time.

- Read the wording carefully. Some words can give you hints to the right answer. There are no exceptions to an answer when there are words in the question such as "always" "all" or "none." If one of the answer choices includes most or some of the right answers, but not all, then that is not the answer. Here is an example:

The primary colors include all of the following:

Red, Yellow, Blue, Green

Red, Green, Yellow

Red, Orange, Yellow

Red, Yellow, Blue

None of the above

- Although item A includes all the right answers, it also includes an incorrect answer, making it incorrect. If you didn't read it carefully, were in a hurry, or didn't know the material well, you might fall for this.

- Make a guess on a question that you do not know the answer to. There is no penalty for an incorrect answer. Eliminate the answer choices that you know are incorrect. For example, this will let your guess be a 1 in 3 chance instead.

 # What Your Score Means

Based on your score, you may, or may not, qualify for credit at your specific institution. At University of Phoenix, a score of 50 is passing for full credit. At Utah Valley University, the score is unpublished, the school will accept credit on a case-by-case basis. Another school, Brigham Young University (BYU) does not accept CLEP credit. To find out what score you need for credit, you need to get that information from your school's website or academic advisor.

You can score between 20 and 80 on any CLEP test. Some exams include percentile ranks. Each correct answer is worth one point. You lose no points for unanswered or incorrect questions. This particular exam is 90 minutes long and has 100 questions.

 # Test Preparation

How much you need to study depends on your knowledge of a subject area. If you are interested in literature, took it in school, or enjoy reading then your study and preparation for the literature or humanities test will not need to be as intensive as that of someone who is new to literature.

This book is much different than the regular CLEP study guides. This book actually teaches you the information that you need to know to pass the test. If you are particularly interested in an area, or feel that you want more information, do a quick search online. We've tried not to include too much depth in areas that are not as essential on the test. It is important to understand all major theories and concepts listed in the table of contents. It is also important to know any bolded words.

Don't worry if you do not understand or know a lot about the area. With minimal study, you can complete and pass the test.

Legal Note

References

[1] ATHERTON J S (2002) Learning and Teaching: Piaget's developmental psychology [On-line]: UK: Available: http://www.dmu.ac.uk/~jamesa/learning/piaget.htm Accessed: 28 March 2003, reprinted with permission.
[2] ATHERTON J S (2002) Learning and Teaching: Piaget's developmental psychology [On-line]: UK: Available: http://www.dmu.ac.uk/~jamesa/learning/piaget.htm Accessed: 28 March 2003, reprinted with permission.
[3] ATHERTON J S (2002) Learning and Teaching: Piaget's developmental psychology [On-line]: UK: Available: http://www.dmu.ac.uk/~jamesa/learning/piaget.htm Accessed: 28 March 2003, reprinted with permission.
[4] Young, Robert G., http://ryoung001.homestead.com/Freud.html Reprinted with permission.

FLASHCARDS

This section contains flashcards for you to use to further your understanding of the material and test yourself on important concepts, names or dates. Read the term or question then flip the page over to check the answer on the back. Keep in mind that this information may not be covered in the text of the study guide. Take your time to study the flashcards, you will need to know and understand these concepts to pass the test.

Wilhelm Wundt

Francis Bacon

Biological Approach

Behavioral Approach

Cognitive Approach

Humanistic

Psychoanalytical

Structuralism

Created Scientific method

First scientific laboratory

Study and observe
behavior - blank slate

Personality is linked to
genetics

All people are inherently
good

How the mind learns and
thinks

Classification of the mind's
structures

Actions are based on
unconscious motivation

Functionalism	Nature vs. Nurture
Variable	Constant
Dependent Variable	Independent Variable
Correlational Research	Clinical Psychologist

Whether or not biology plays a part in personality

William James - the "how" part of behavior

A variable that always stays the same

A changing part of the person

The variables that the experimenter controls

The variable the experiment is trying to get information about

Doctoral degree in Psychology, cannot prescribe medicine

How much one variable changes in relation to each other

Psychiatrist

Ethics

Hypothalamus

Autonomic Nervous System

Sympathetic Nervous System

Parasympathetic Nervous System

Limbic System

Hippocampus

Principals and standards of behavior including morals

A medical doctor with a degree in Psychotherapy, can prescribe drugs

Involuntary system

Part of the endocrine system

Calming part of the system

Arousing part of the system

Stores memories

Memory and emotion center

Cerebral Cortex

Occipital Lobe

Temporal Lobe

Frontal Lobe

Parietal Lobe

Cerebrum

Cerebellum

Pons

Vision

Most developed and largest part of the brain

Voluntary muscles and intelligence

Hearing

The two large halves of the brain

Body sensations

Control breathing and heart rate

Coordinates all movements and muscles

Brain Stem

Thalamus

Hypothalamus

Gregor Mendel

Somatic Cell

Cloning

Gametes

Zygote

Main relay station for
sensory signals

Sends commands to all
other parts of the body

Father of genetics

Regulates internal
temperature

Reproduction done with
just the somatic cell

A full set of chromosomes

First part of a human

Reproductive cells (eggs
and sperm)

Vestibular Sense

Absolute Threshold

Sclera

Iris

Pupil

Cornea

Lens

Retina

How much sensation
one has to have to feel
something

Balance and body
movement

Colored part of the eye

White part of the eye

A clear membrane that
protects the eye

Part of the eye that is
black, opens and closes to
let in light

Back of the eye. Contains
rods and cones.

Transparent and located in
front of the eye

Cones

Noise

Frequency

Pitch

Amplitude

Loudness

Timbre

Outer Ear

Irrelevant stimuli that competes for attention

Use to view color

Ear's interpretation of a sound's frequency

The number of full wavelengths that pass through a point in a given amount of time

A sound wave's amplitude

Amount of pressure produced by a sound wave and is measured in decibels

Includes pinna and external auditory canal

The perceptual quality of sound

Middle Ear

Inner Ear

Cochlea

Organ of Corti

Gestalt Psychology

Depth Perception

Visual Cliff

Erik Erickson

Oval window, cochlea, organ of Corti

Eardrum, anvil, stirrup

A part of the ear inside the cochlea

A fluid filled structure in the inner ear that looks like a snail

Makes people see objects in three dimensions

People organize their perceptions by patterns

Psychoanalyst

Proof that babies have depth perception

Most important thing to Erickson

Trust vs. Mistrust

Autonomy vs. Shame and Doubt

Initiative vs. Guilt

Industry vs. Inferiority

Identity vs. Role Confusion

Intimacy vs. Isolation

Generativity vs. Stagnation

Infant

Development of trust

Preschooler

Toddler

Adolescent

School-Age

Middle-Age Adult

Young Adult

Ego Integrity vs. Despair

Jean Piaget

Accommodation

Classification

Class Inclusion

Conservation

Developmental Norm

Egocentrism

Cognitive theorist	Old age
The ability to group objects together on a basis of common features	The difference made to one's mind or concepts by the process of assimilation
The realization that objects or sets of objects stay the same even when they are changed about or made to look different	The understanding of more advanced than simple classification, that some classes or sets of objects are also sub-sets of a larger class
The belief that you are the center of the universe and everything revolves around you	A statistical measure of typical scores for categories of information

Elaboration

Operation

Recognition

Recall

Schema

Stage

**Reflexive Stage
(0-2 months)**

**Primary Circular
Reactions
(2-4 months)**

The process of working
something out in your head

Relating new information to
something familiar

Being able to reproduce
knowledge from memory

The ability to identify
correctly something
encountered before

A period in a child's
development in which
he or she is capable of
understanding some things
but not others

The representation in
the mind of a set of
perceptions, ideas, and/or
actions, which go together

Reflexive behaviors occur
in stereotyped repetition
such as opening and
closing fingers repetitively

Simple reflex activity such
as grasping and sucking

Secondary Circular Reactions (4-8 months)

Coordination of Secondary Reactions (8-12 months)

Tertiary Circular Reactions (12-18 months)

Invention of New Means Through Mental Combination (18-12 months)

Preoperational Phase (2-4 years)

Intuitive Phase (4-7 years)

Period of Concrete Operations (7-11 years)

Period of Formal Operation (11-15 years)

Responses become coordinated into more complex sequences. Actions take on an "intentional" character.

Repetition of change actions to reproduce interesting consequences such as kicking one's feet to move a mobile suspended over the crib

Evidence of an internal representational system. Symbolizing the problem-solving sequence before actually responding. Deferred imitation.

Discovery of new ways to produce the same consequence or obtain the same goal such as the infant may pull a pillow toward him in an attempt to get a toy resting on it

Speech becomes more social, less egocentric. The child has an intuitive grasp of logical concepts in some areas.

Increased use of verbal representation but speech is egocentric. The beginnings of symbolic rather than simple motor play.

Though becomes more abstract, incorporating the principles of formal logic. The ability to generate abstract propositions, multiple hypotheses and their possible outcomes is evident.

Evidence for organized, logical thought. There is the ability to perform multiple classification tasks, order objects in a logical sequence, and comprehend the principle of conservation.

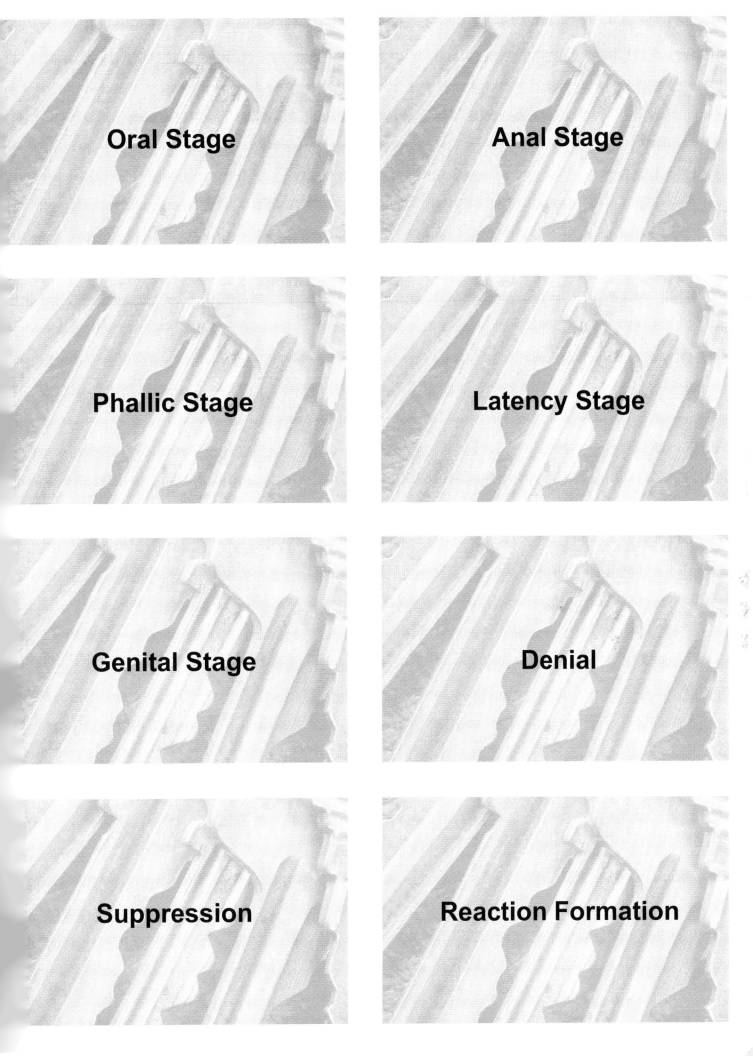

Oral Stage

Anal Stage

Phallic Stage

Latency Stage

Genital Stage

Denial

Suppression

Reaction Formation

1-3 Years

Birth-1 year

6-11 Years

3-6 Years

Complete rejection of the feeling or situation

Adolescence

Turning a feeling into the exact opposite feeling. For example, saying you hate someone you are interested in.

Hiding the feelings and no acknowledging them

Projection

Displacement

Rationalization

Regression

Sublimation

Self-actualization

Esteem Needs

Belonging and Love

Feelings are redirected to someone else. Someone who has a bad day at work and can't complain goes home and yells at their kids instead.

Projection is transferring your thoughts and feelings onto others. For example, someone who is being unfaithful themselves constantly accuses their partner of cheating.

Reverting to old behavior to avoid feelings

You deny your feelings and come up with ways to justify your behavior

Highest need in hierarchy - Level 5

A type of displacement, redirection of the feeling into a socially productive activity

Level 3 need

Level 4 need

Safety

Physical Needs

Operant Conditioning

Instructional Conditioning

Extinction

Egocentric Behavior

Social Learning Theory

Baby Albert

Level 1 need

Level 2 need

Gives a negative sanction

Reinforces good behavior

A child does not take
into consideration other
people's needs

The process of
unassociating the condition
with the response

Was kept in a box and
conditioned

Explicit role instruction
(stereotypes), boys play
with trucks and cars, girls
wear make-up

Stimulus Generalization

Naturalistic Observation

Id

Ego

Super Ego

Visual Cliff

Object Permanence

Harry Harlow

Search conducted by watching the subject

Something from conditioning carries over to another related area

The mediator between ego and id

Primitive part of the subconscious which wants food and sex

Experiment to prove infants have depth perception

Ethical, super good part of the subconscious

Monkey experiment - monkeys liked the soft one better

Understanding that an object does not cease to exist once it has left your vision

Who made the first IQ test?

Formula to find out IQ?

Hyperactivity affects what percentage of children?

Divergent Thinking

Convergent Thinking

Naturalistic Observation

Independent Variable

Cross-Sectional Studies

IQ = Mental Age/
Calculated Age x 100

Alfred Binet

Creative process of
thinking

0.03

Search conducted by
watching the subject

Follower thinking

When people of different
ages are studied at one
particular time

The one the researchers
have direct control over

Longitudinal Studies	Quantitative
Qualitative	Four Steps of the Scientific Method
Kohberg's Theory of Moral Development	Preconventional Morality
Conventional Morality	Postconventional Morality

The number or amount of something

Where the people are followed over a long period of time and checked up on at certain points

Gather information, generate hypothesis, test hypothesis, revise

Used in statistics, similar in structure or organization

Punishment of obedience phase

How morality is linked to behavior

Motivation is because law is a higher order

Motivation to obey is done from influence of other people

Made in the USA
Columbia, SC
10 December 2021

50922354R00078